Sally,
God Bless and Thanx!
Nat Parks

A SINGLE TOMORROW IN A LAND OF YESTERDAYS

∽

by

Neal Brandan Parks

xulon PRESS

Copyright © 2006 by Neal Brandan Parks

A Single Tomorrow in a Land of Yesterdays
by Neal Brandan Parks

Printed in the United States of America

ISBN 1-60034-631-6

All rights reserved solely by the author. The author guarantees all contents are original and do not infringe upon the legal rights of any other person or work. No part of this book may be reproduced in any form without the permission of the author. The views expressed in this book are not necessarily those of the publisher.

Bible quotations are taken from **The Full Life Study Bible — New International Version**. Copyright © 1992 by Life Publishers International.

www.xulonpress.com

Contents

Poems

Salvation 11
   Salvation conceived *13*
   Glory Revealed *15*
   Beaten, Not Broken *16*
   The Battlefield *18*
   Reach Me *20*
   You Thought of Me *22*
   Bring Death *24*
   Measure of Evil *25*
   Unto Your Hand *28*
   The Story *29*
   Gray *30*
   Through *31*
   Turn to Him *32*
   What died *34*
   Letting Go *36*

Deliverance 39
   Death Designed *41*
   Deceiver *42*
   How Is It? *44*
   My Shield and Sword *45*
   Dawn *46*

In the Light *47*
Through Death *48*
The Long Way *50*
Against All Odds *52*
Broken Waters *53*
Shadow of Death *54*
Running *55*
Fallen Ones *57*
Escape *59*
The Flame *61*
Sweet Release *63*
For Which Light is Named *64*
My Avenger *66*
How Dare You *68*
Dealings of Death *70*

Praise **71**
Champion *73*
By Your Hand *74*
Lord of Glory *76*
Glorious *78*
Praises *79*
Sufficient *81*
If I Could Paint Like You *82*
Eternal *84*
Provider *86*
My Hands *88*
The One of Abundant Worth *90*
Master *91*
My Thanks *93*
The Test *94*
My God and King *96*
In Awe *98*
Thank You *100*

Christian Life **101**
Your Way *103*

Freedom Reign, Freedom Ring *105*
Never *107*
Come Back! *109*
The King's Armor *110*
Nothing *112*
My Nation, My People *114*
Shall Never Yield *116*
No Excuse *117*

Renewal **119**
   Deepen Me *121*
   The Sun *122*
   Here *123*
   My Pledge *124*
   The Attack *125*
   Fortress *127*
   I Pray *128*
   Arrogance Will Pass *129*
   Something Holy *131*
   Renew *132*
   Of Peace, Love, and Joy *134*
   Closer *136*
   Formed Anew *138*

Heaven **139**
   Everlasting Paradise *141*
   Find Him *143*
   They Must Know *144*
   Tribute *145*
   My Reward *147*
   The Trumpet and Its Thunder *148*
   One Day *149*
   All Who See *150*
   The Promise Beyond *152*

Love **155**
   Your Words *157*

I Have Loved You *158*
Infinite Love *160*
Pure Love *162*
Silence Speaks *164*
Companion *165*
Do You Know *167*
Of My Dream *168*
The Jewel *170*
Allow Me *172*
The Gift *174*
I Do *176*
Life in Love *177*

Children **179**
Treasure of Mine *181*
Blessed Emergence *182*
Smiles Returned *183*
No Claim *184*

Stories

I Met a Man *187*
The Boy at the Altar *193*
Only a Boy *197*
The Healer *203*
The Old Man and the King *207*
Strange Comfort *221*
Thirteen *229*
The Valley *237*

This book is dedicated to:
All who have been supportive throughout this endeavor,
Dear friends and family—especially my wife, Melissa;
My children, Nolan and Elanor; and above all,
Jesus Christ—my Lord, Savior, and Deliverer.

SALVATION

SALVATION CONCEIVED

Mourning their fallen King,
From eleven fearful faces
Bittersweet memories pouring
Upon dark and hidden places.
Steadfast faith left behind,
Faded promises long forgotten;
Unbroken, but lost in darkened minds—
With His death passed their resolution!

The story of their fallen King;
Two days fallen from their tongues,
The story of their Lord revealing
The Blessed Kingdom come—
In declarations of power and glory,
They beheld their Servant Lord
Obedient to the foretold story,
And were dismayed by death and sword!

Remembering their fallen King,
Clouded minds born of man,
Overrun by Darkness' spring,
Ever forgetting His great plan:
Rescue from death purchased by death—
The Holy One's blood spilt—
Giving to all His last breath,
For Holy Communion rebuilt!

Was He only a fallen king—
Susceptible to torture and death?
Of whom songs would sing,
And generations be blessed;
Were His healing hands of mere flesh?
Was there more to Him than they saw?
God and man in perfect mesh—
In He who bore no flaw!

continued

A Single Tomorrow in a Land of Yesterdays

Mourning their fallen King,
Hope borne free from stony tomb,
Earth and Heaven rejoicing sing
Of God's plan in full bloom.
Upon the stone, empty cloths laid,
He is risen, and fear is relieved;
In hearts where darkness played,
Salvation now conceived!

Rejoicing their risen King,
Steadfast faith now reborn,
Hope to the masses He brings,
Powers of Sin, Death, and Hell now torn.
To His throne now returned,
The King resumes His rightful place,
Darkness eternally overturned,
His blood bought the human race!

GLORY REVEALED

Where is your glory
In this dark and discontented earth?
Men curse your name,
The Name above all names,
And shake their fists at heaven.
"Where are you now?"
They ask in defiant disregard,
"There is no God!"
They proclaim with insane ignorance!
Bring wisdom upon them sharply,
Make your power known,
For they have cursed you far too long!
They seek freedom from conviction,
Meanwhile heaping fuel on the Fire of doom!
They build fortresses for security
Out of leaves and twigs,
But soon it will be cast down and destroyed,
Let them hear the thunder of your voice, O Lord,
Before time runs out!
Awake them from their false security,
Show to them their appointed doom:
All knees will bow at your Throne of Judgment!
Reveal your power to the multitudes
Of the misled and misguided,
Let them see what will come
Despite their deceptive hope in their own righteousness.
For there is not one who is worthy of pardon,
Not one who will avoid just judgment,
Bring them before you now,
Before all is lost!
Call your children home, Dear Lord,
Break the curse of your blind people,
Bring them forth out of the Distant Darkness
Into your revealing presence,
Where all is laid bare!
Show them your unseen glory!

BEATEN, NOT BROKEN

Words cannot describe the pain—
You, my Lord, came as King,
Stood trial for innocence,
Were beaten as a criminal,
Loved your enemies more than self
Love stronger than emotion,
Selfless beyond compare.
You, my Lord,
Endured pain upon pain
For the good of those that killed you,
Offered them life,
Refusing, they condemned your purity.
Sentenced to death,
You freely gave your body,
To be crushed,
In agony—
Beaten, not broken,
Still possessed your power.
Power in love, not in strength,
Yet strength it was,
Sought only their forgiveness
The spikes pierced your holy flesh,
Holy Father turned His back to you,
The sins of all the world were upon you.
And still you sought our freedom—
Pain made us free,
Death gave us life,
Your demise was our redemption,
Your blood our sacrifice.
The pain you bore for us,
Paid all our debts.

The keys of hell you took for us
For you were beaten, not broken,
Still possessing your power,
Power in love,
Power in strength,
Forgiveness and freedom.

A Single Tomorrow in a Land of Yesterdays

THE BATTLEFIELD

This fight for man's salvation
Upon life's battlefield,
Stained red with blood,
Many wounded,
Many dead,
All lives changed
By this thing called war,
A once peaceful landscape,
Ravaged and torn
By man's self-destruction,
Why don't they heed the call?
The battlefield cries out,
"Look to the sky, you fools,
Your Savior is waiting"

Men bent on hatred,
On sin,
On death,
Ignoring the call,
Vengeance is their desire,
Murder—their plan,
Still the blood flows
On and on,
It pours out
Until all is laid waste,
And still man desires more,
And the battlefield cries out,
"Look to heaven, you fools,
There is your peace"

All creation warns them
The King will return,
And still they fight for nothing,
Receiving only pain,
And turmoil,

And anguish,
Will they not stop?
They cannot please themselves,
They must turn their eyes
From the lowliness
To the heavens above,
So the battlefield cries out,
"Seek the savior, you fools,
His name is Mighty"

Time continues without delay,
Proceeding for the King's coming,
Men seek the end yet fear it,
For death is no end,
It is only the beginning
What is to fear?
Life comes from Him,
Freely he gives it,
So receive it now,
Without delay,
Without doubt,
And the battlefield cries out,
"Come to Jesus, you fools,
Give Him your hearts"

REACH ME

In the shadows,
I am worn by the indomitable—
The depths of my own destructive force.
I highly esteem
All the creatures that creep and crawl
Midst the filth!
Arising unseen, I search the paths of darkness;
Beyond the extended arm of sunlight, and moonlight,
I wander endlessly,
Echoes of love, peace and rest
Torment my every whistling breath.
The rise and fall of my chest
Is a writhing of my chained and shackled heart!

To the One I have not seen I cry out,
"Reach me!"

Too busy to await His reply,
I carry on—
Searching in the unbreakable blackness
For the Lighted Way!
My struggle through the darkness
Seems to have only begun.
Walls that were once faithful and strong,
My support through the gloom of yesterdays,
Have found themselves victims
Of their own misguided fury.
The rubble of toppled rock and brick,
Clutters my already disheveled path!
My body aches,
My heart and soul yearn
For a single breath of peace and comfort!
My descent has clouded my mind,
And I stand breathless, gasping, in the Depths of my Destruction!

To the One I have not seen I cry out,
"Reach me!"
Is my voice is too weak
Or my Rescuer too far away?
"Your voice has not fallen on deaf ears."
My heart lifted by His soothing voice,
"Long have I watched your path.
You have searched long enough, my child.
Let the search end here
For I am the source of what you seek,
You will see the light unveiled,
And my glory revealed, for I have reached you!"

YOU THOUGHT OF ME

Born to a virgin
To free the world from sin,
You thought of me.

Lord of Glory
Wrapped in human flesh,
You thought of me.

Raised from childhood
By parents you created,
You thought of me.

Lord of Hosts
Despised and mistreated,
You thought of me.

Holy and blameless
Hated by your own priests,
You thought of me.

Accused by men
Of blaspheming yourself,
You thought of me.

You thought of me,
As they beat and mocked you,
These men you formed in the womb,
You knew what you had to do,
Even take your love to the tomb.
You were spit upon and cursed,
Denied by your own creation,
But that was not the worst,
When you paid for our insurrection.

You took our failures to hell,
And stole the power of sin,
You loosed me from my eternal cell,
Freedom you gave when you rose again.

BRING DEATH

I offer to you, my Lord,
My life.
I give it freely,
And I beg you, "Take it."
Bring death to me,
So I might have true life.
This life of my own
Is nothing.
I have sought many things
On my own,
And never do I attain them!
Bring death to me,
To my dreams,
To my worldly plans.
I must die to self,
And to sin.
All the paths I have chosen
Lead nowhere.
Those paths only
Distract attention from the One Truth!
This is the truth:
I must die to self,
And to sin.
In Jesus Christ
Is the life, true life
That I have always sought.
So, Lord Jesus,
Bring death to me!
Make me your child,
And bring death
To my evil, sinful nature.
For through this death
Is the path to eternal life!

MEASURE OF EVIL

Wickedness flows in us all,
All we see,
All we hear and smell,
And all we touch—
All things perceived
Must first pass through our flesh,
It is our link to this world,
Our demise in the next!
Controlling thoughts and dreams,
It pollutes and deceives,
Seeking only momentary pleasure,
Forgetting the promised end.
It desires deeply to be master,
Itself deceived
By the creator of lies,
The pleasure is short-lived,
Followed by endless misery and destruction!
The flesh,
Chained and addicted,
Writhes to rebel against rebellion,
Steals hope from soul and spirit,
Twisting and turning,
Chains tighten, choking life away!
For the chains increase,
Adding addiction to addiction,
Evil upon evil,
We all are born with a measure of evil,
Our flesh—
The very nature we are born in—
Is our nemesis!
It loathes control,
Glories in misconduct,
Seeking worldly gain,
And mocking spiritual renewal!

continued

A Single Tomorrow in a Land of Yesterdays

As a trap it displays its lure,
Looking pure and right,
Hurting no one,
No one except for the fool,
The fool crushed by the vise-like jaws!
Gloating and triumphing in pain,
Pleasure vanishes instantly,
Never to return,
The flesh sees no other master,
And is terribly deceived!
For there stands one above it,
One who longs,
Desires to multiply the measure of evil,
For evil is his plan for all,
Yet his power,
Just as his evil,
Will soon come to pass!
For we were born with a spirit-man,
With that spirit we find escape,
Freedom from the nature
That leads only to death.
He has eyes to see what the flesh cannot,
There is a light beyond the darkness,
A hope to all captives,
An end to all storms,
A joy midst cries of anguish,
A key to all chains,
An answer to all prayers,
And a Savior to all sinners!
He gives an abundant measure of good
To shred all remnants of evil,
Darkness flees His presence,
And chains drop broken at His feet,
He brings life to death,
Hope to the hopeless,
Peace to the tormented,
And freedom to slaves!

His name is Jesus, Savior of all men!
He is a warrior, mighty in battle,
All must pledge loyalty,
Or be struck down,
None can stand before Him as enemy,
The master of evil
Cringes in His mighty presence!
He is glorious and beautiful,
Frightening and terrible to all evil,
He is Jesus,
Flesh obeys Him, and evil flees in haste,
He is God, and Savior,
Bringer of peace and hope and love,
Forgiver of sins,
Lover of sinners,
Commander of the Host of Heaven,
Master of all,
King of Kings,
He is Jesus, Savior of all men!

UNTO YOUR HAND

You have given faith
To faint not,
To rise above the wicked plot.

You have given joy
Unlooked for,
To weather the windy shore.

You have given love
Unconditionally,
To accept all into your family.

You have given wisdom
For paths unknown,
To choose the Way to your Throne.

You have given mercy
Unwarranted,
To cleanse souls tainted.

You gave yourself
Willingly,
To redeem and set free!

I give myself
Unworthily,
And thank you, God, unceasingly!

I give my all
To your command,
To bring your people unto your hand!

THE STORY

There is a story common to all men,
All tribes, nations, and colors of men,
A story of grief and sorrow,
Immeasurable treasure lost!
Though all have sought for it,
All have wrongfully searched,
This treasure is no longer hidden in deep places,
It is not buried in a locked box,
It has been revived,
It has ascended to High Ground,
Look up you seekers of treasure,
For the ground cannot contain One of this value!
You will not find it in worldly realms,
Seeking beneath earth,
Look up!
For it is plain to see,
Its glory shines all around,
Put down your shovels!
The earthly treasures you have found
Do not compare to the One,
Turn your eyes from your mounds of gold and silver,
And seek the One,
The One whose worth is not measured in dollars,
But in eternal riches!
Forget what you have found,
Those treasures too quickly pass,
They are fleeting and unrewarding,
Turn your focus on the true and eternal,
The One Treasure!

A Single Tomorrow in a Land of Yesterdays

GRAY

Since the foundations of earth were laid
There were two kingdoms,
Incessantly they strive,
One against the other.
When the world was created
In the Light and Power of God,
Those that dwell ever in Darkness
Sought to destroy it,
And mold it into a kingdom of blindness.
And the Battle for the Sake of Men ensued,
The dark ones took light,
Lacking power to create,
Misshaped it and released it as their own creation,
Fooling all the races of men!
For men seek the Light,
Looking for a way out of the Dark,
And finding the grayness between, are utterly deceived!
Forsaking their search for true light,
They become content in the gray gloom.
Awake, you foolish men, and behold the Light!
The grayness is but a mockery of the True Light,
It is a diluted light,
Diluted by the Kingdom of Darkness!
Forsake this compromise!
Abandon the doom of eternal torment!
Turn unto the light,
Or face it and be ashamed of your sins forever!
For the True Light will come again,
And He will judge those who dwell in the Gray and the Dark,
For there are only two kingdoms;
Seek out the Light and you will find it,
Or you will be doomed forever!

THROUGH

I lack strength to continue,
I fail in all I attempt to do,
I cannot stand on my own feet,
And now, certain is my defeat.
When all seems lost and gone,
You pick me up and carry me on,
When all hope has left my side,
You love me as your bride.
Why with you do I despair?
I should walk through without care.
The battle is already won,
It was over before it begun.
My rear guard is you,
Blocking all that would get through.
With you I will not stop,
I plan to reach the top.
All, you say, is given me,
Guaranteed the victory!
My life I owe to you,
For all you have brought me through.
You carried me through the battlefield,
You took my sword, you were my shield!
I will not cease in loving you,
Though my short life be through.
I remain in you, for all eternity,
Forever you will stay with me!

TURN TO HIM

There is no escape,
You are everywhere,
And you see everything;
Nothing can hide
From your eyes and ears.
You know all,
Perceive all,
Understand all things.
Why do I run from you?
Nowhere can I hide,
Nowhere can I avoid your love.
Through time I run
Seeking freedom from you,
Yet true freedom
Is found only in you!
I flee you at my own peril.

It is truly dangerous,
To flee the Almighty God.
None can escape His love,
Though countless many have tried,
Only to endure hardship
Through all time,
And all eternity.
None have escaped God,
And none have escaped His final judgment!
Who can hide from the Almighty?
Turn to embrace Him,
In Him are all treasures,
Every kind of riches,
And all power is at His command!

None can prepare themselves to meet Him,
There is only one guide
Who leads to the Lord's presence.
Follow Him through all troubles,
And have faith;
He will bring you through!

WHAT DIED

Our hatred He bore with bitter imprint upon His back,
Solemn sorrow and the Sufferer's Way—
Walking in innocence, the Insolents' pardon did lack—
No reprieve from the murderous mob today!
With malice and mockery we murdered Him there,
With spurn and spite we raised Him up,
The sight of His tattered and torn body few could bear,
This man born to bear His Father's cup.
I testify, this man called King, His death sure and certain,
My spear I did plunge—pierce His side,
Mountain and meadow and sky, rending the temple curtain,
Mourned the man who died—crucified!
That day a Savior died!
Burdened and buried with Death, He was not forever forsaken,
Now Solitude's shadow swiftly to us
Brought grief and fear the hour our hopes and hatred were taken,
O, what they had tortuously taken from us!
That day the Savior died!

That day shall surely, undeniably, be forever named: Good!
Shadows briefly settled ere the sun should rise,
The day He descended where Shadows thought He never would,
All would be surprised at the foretold sunrise!
Entombed where their Lord should be,
were discovered Death and Destiny,
A bold and burning light they also found,
"Ladies, look not here, the Son has risen,
displaying His light for all to see."
And where their faces fell they found Holy Ground!
Through Death He rose, righteous and unopposed,
forever enthroned,
Bearing still the scars of the Sufferer's Way,
Beyond doubt or disbelief He stood,
no longer dishonored and disowned,
He arose for all who pierced Him along the Way!

Love conquered Death that day!
Death, disease, religion, Hell,
and sin passed away when He rose again,
Now the Holy Spirit's sudden swift fire
Brought to us that same power—pertinacious power—
to destroy sin,
Hail the Lord and risen King, Bringer of Holy Fire!
Praises to the Conqueror of Death!

LETTING GO

Finally, at the altar I stand,
Facing painful truth,
Realizing who I truly am,
I look into your deep-revealing eyes,
And all is laid bare before you.
Facing the King of Kings
I face all crimes committed,
And all pain,
Given and received,
Now I know the depths of my fall;
I have caused pain unbearable,
And death unalterable,
In His mirroring eyes I see all,
And know that I am the criminal,
Knowingly committed,
I clung to my precious crimes.
But here I stand,
Drawn to you, my Holy Judge,
In the light of your smiling countenance,
I give it up,
And lay it down,
Letting go.
All my life has led me here, for this time,
And now I weep,
My stone heart falls, your mercy complete.
Now I see it clearly,
This thing I held so tightly, for so long,
As it falls from my trembling hand
I give it up,
And lay it down,
I let it go!
The very thing that brought your pain, and death,
Was my secret companion,
Now revealed:
Three blood stained spikes, and one spiteful hammer!

I confess: I caused your pain, your death,
I drove the nails,
But now I ask for mercy, for undeserved pardon,
Forgive me, my Lord God!
I give it up,
And lay it down,
Letting go!

DELIVERANCE

DEATH DESIGNED

From what I run, I dare not say.
I fear its return before the end of the day,
Long have I fought and struggled with it,
Deep are my scars; my heart it has bit!
Like the cold chill of Winter's Wind,
It freezes my soul and cuts through the skin.
As a knife pierces flesh its tip drives into my soul,
It desires only death and destruction—complete and whole!
The teeth I fear, the bite I dread,
It's as though I am already dead!
My death seems sure, my life complete,
"Is there no one I cannot beat",
I hear the ghastly voice mock its new victim,
But his victory is the one I gave him.
I see it now though is it too late?
I set the table and made my own plate.
The deadly bite, the vicious teeth,
My sure death, my life complete,
My Enemy's weapons are not his own design,
I gave them freely, for they our mine!
I am my own demise,
I gave him his very prize!
My soul he has sought from my life's beginning,
And from that point he has designed the ending!
Though his plans are now revealed,
My death and destruction are not sealed!
There is a way to defeat him soundly!
To accept God as King, and accept Him proudly,
Now Death has lost his grip, and his teeth have no sting,
For by my death my life He brings!
No cold do I fear; no bite do I dread,
For in my enemy's haste I have crushed his vile head!

DECEIVER

Though the Deceiver is strong,
You are exceedingly stronger,
Though he seeks to ruin your people,
You have already freed them
From his deception.
His power to deceive—
Allowed by you
Until the appointed time,
A time when evil is annihilated,
And you, O Lord, take back
The power lent to our Enemy.
His power is not his own,
He has no power except what you allow.
So Lord, we eagerly await
Your judgment of him!
Make it swift and decisive,
Crush him in your right hand,
In the same merciless way
He would crush your servants!
For you are just and holy,
When it begins
Allow us to watch the Evil One taken
And crushed in your hand;
All who have sinned,
Deceived by him,
Long for his destruction.
The deceiver has been deceived,
By his own plot.
You are our avenger,
Let justice be done by your mighty hand,
Snuff out his vile plot, O Lord,
And burn his horde—a pile of refuse!

O Lord, you are sovereign,
This band of rebels would contaminate your creation,
And defile your children!
Take out your justice on them, O Lord,
And let them tremble in fear of your mighty vengeance!

HOW IS IT?

How is it that death undeserved
Brings life undeserved?
How is it that one man dies
That all men, after, might have life?
How is it that through His suffering
All are freed from torment and pain?
How is it that this gift is freely given,
When it was bought with the ultimate price?
How is it that sin is forgiven and forgotten
Though all men deserve the doom of death and hell?

Our demise is undone,
Our death is atoned for,
Our Destroyer is destroyed,
Our Deceiver is thrown down,
And all penalties are paid in full!
By the One who answers all questions.

He has done all things,
The Savior, Creator, and Lover of all people
Suffered and died
In agony and pain undeniable,
And through that death all have life,
Answers to all questions,
And freedom from inevitable doom!

MY SHIELD AND SWORD

Your word is powerful,
I cling to it,
It is my shield,
My sword,
My light through all trials.
Spoken from on high,
It reaches to the depths
Of my soul,
To guide,
To direct,
And to carry me on my journey.
Your word marks my path,
I cling to it,
Amidst all things it stands alone,
Calling for all to hear,
Telling of the Mighty One,
Lighting the way to Him!
Though the path is beaten
I know the way,
It is plain before me,
Distinct its markings;
Your word leads through,
Through all battles,
Valleys and peaks,
Straight to your side!
Your word is powerful,
I cling to it,
It is my shield,
My sword,
My light through all trials.
It will bring me through!

DAWN

Signifying what will come to pass,
A new day begins with dawn,
All blindness of night
Overcome by the rising sun.
Through its power of light
Darkness vanishes,
And the world is revealed.
This points to the future—
The future all men share—
When evil is destroyed forever!
For there comes a day
When the Mighty Son will rise,
And darkness will not endure
His awesome light!
A new age will dawn—
An age of peace,
An age of rejoicing,
An age that will never cease;
The blindness of night
Will never return.
We will see all there is to see,
Basking in the light of
His holy presence.
A new Heaven, and a new Earth
Will be our home.
Its walls will be His love.
The Enemy banished,
His throne of power cast down;
Replaced by Almighty God!
Forever will our yoke of darkness
Be broken,
And forever will our blindness
Be lifted by His light!

IN THE LIGHT

I carry with me
All my internal darkness.
I have desired for so long
To find freedom from this ever-growing burden.
It grows like a cancer in my soul!
Why has your presence evaded me?
I realize now that you do not evade,
It is that I must flee your presence
Because of this sin I carry!
Why is it so difficult to lay it down?
It is only a burden,
And a plague,
Yet I cling to it like lost treasure!
My treasure it has become,
My own very worthless treasure.
Help me; help me
To release it!
My steps are labored
Under the stress of my enormous burden.
I require strength,
Strength that is not my own.
I see the essence
Of the power in which I seek.
It is a light,
A tremendous and bright light.
My burden seems to shrink in its glow,
And I run with all speed
To bathe in its brightness!
My burden is washed away in the tide.
The source of the light
Revealed in a mighty voice:
"Welcome home, my son."
I hear you say!

THROUGH DEATH

Through death He came,
Seemingly defeated He breathed his last,
Yet beyond death and the grave—
Beyond the curse of sin He came
To the very lair of Satan—
For He had a penalty to pay,
The price was not His to bear,
Yet bear it He must,
All the future of creation depending on that penalty!

Through Hell He came,
Seemingly defeated by the hands of Satan,
Yet beyond Hell and its gates He came,
Beyond the chains of Hell's dungeon He rose,
Triumphant He rose!
And all sin he conquered with His spilled blood,
The price was not His, nor the pain endured,
Yet He bore it for our redemption,
And took from Satan the keys to all that binds us to our sin!

You, Lord, have blessed us beyond all hopes,
Beyond all curses,
All chains and prisons,
Beyond all pains and death,
But most of all, beyond the penalty of our sins!
And for that we give you our lives,
And our deaths;
Use us to perform your will,
To bring freedom to those who are still bound,
For you came through Death and Hell,
You conquered Satan in his own kingdom,
You rose to give life freely,
And for that reason we live for you!

To Him we owe an enormous debt of gratitude,
Yet from us all He wants is love!
We owe Him our very existence,
And all He asks for is faith in Him as Lord of All!

THE LONG WAY

Been down this road too many times,
The straighter it goes the more it winds.
It sweeps away from the road I sought,
In its tangled web I am caught.
Been on this path for far too long,
It drags me down and steals my song.
Like a predator, it lured me here,
In its vicious jaws it is all too clear.

I have traveled the wrong way,
I have left my path.
Save me today,
Or forever I will stay in your wrath!

Been down this way too many times,
The longer I stay the more it blinds.
All my sight has failed me today,
Which way from here, I cannot say.
All seems lost in this barren land,
Sinking below the burning sand.
The Truth walks not on my chosen road,
Alone I travel with my burdensome load.

I have traveled the wrong way,
I have left my path.
Save me today,
Or forever I will stay in your wrath!

Been too long since I have been on my knees,
The longer I stand the harder I fall, it seems.
On my knees, my sight is returned instantly,
With my pleas, I am saved completely
From the snares that would entrap me here, or there;
You gave the wings to fly, to soar through the air!

I found the Right Path and the Truth is on hand,
He is my guide through this barren, burning land!

I have traveled the long way,
I have left the Forbidden Path.
I am saved today,
And forever, from your wrath!

AGAINST ALL ODDS

Lord, my triumph is in you!
For your spirit lives within,
And with it I am invincible.
When all is stacked against me,
And the Enemy attacks in full force,
You hand me the victory.
You, O Lord, are my guard,
And you stand by me in battle.
For with you,
And against all odds
I rejoice,
For I have been redeemed;
Pulled back
From the edge of destruction.
You, my Savior, set me free.
My companion you are,
And you take away all fears!
I am surrounded by you,
Your right arm
Is my very great protector!
All enemies are struck down,
And destroyed
By your right hand, my Lord!
For with you,
And against all odds
I rejoice,
For I have been redeemed—
Pulled back
From the edge of destruction!

BROKEN WATERS

With many thoughts of times lost,
My mind must swim
Oceans of half-forgotten paths—
Memory-faded paths—
To find an island of peace
Amidst the broken waters.

Seldom does the land stand still;
Tossing my battered
And torn heart back to the waters—
Diseased waters of memory—
Sworn memories time-faded
Amidst the broken waters.

Questions crash in a torrent
Upon my forlorn heart,
Why must I stand alone?
Alone with painful fading memories,
Of joy, happiness, and love
Amidst the broken waters.

With the rise and fall of well-known waves,
Mind-numbing pain
Becomes my loathsome friend—
Companion and captor—
Blind to all but him
Amidst the broken waters.

A familiar hand reaching for me,
A rescue unlooked for
From my depression—
Painful loss and forgotten memory—
To a land safe and sound
Amidst the broken waters.

SHADOW OF DEATH

The sun sinks slowly
Behind the purple mountain.
The forest blanketed
By darkness and shadow.
Trees take on faces,
Ageless faces,
Disfigured by malice.
The mountain,
No longer purple —
Distorted by the blackened sky.
All around, the shadows grow —
Shadows of death
And demise.
Menacing they are,
As a land without light.
Every rustling,
Of the leafless branches,
Inspires fear and fright.
Fear is rooted in darkness,
But I carry the light!
Light exposes
Those frightful images,
And they flee.
Light abides not in darkness,
And darkness flees its mighty presence.
Shadows hold no weapons,
And darkness fights no battle,
It is only a coward.
So take up the light,
And fear not!
For light gives free passage
Through the blackened night.

RUNNING

Running,
I dare not look back,
My past seeks to destroy,
All I have gained
Would be lost.

The past,
Dark and dangerous,
Pleasures in pain.
From it I flee,
Seeking refuge.

Pursuing,
With reckless abandon,
To steal and kill,
Life and freedom,
Bringing downfall.

Running,
I do not look back,
My past seeks to destroy,
All I have gained
Would be lost.

The past
Has been defeated,
No power it holds,
I have lived it once,
And return no more!

Pursuing,
With all strength,
Abandoning weakness,
Forgetting pain,
Seeking the Giver of Life.

continued

Running,
I dare not look back,
What I need is before me,
All to gain,
In His presence!

FALLEN ONES

Dangerous are the fallen ones, called demons,
Treacherous is their leader,
Who exalted himself over God.
You, O Lord, created them all,
You know them by name
And in the end you will destroy them.

Thank you, Lord, for the promised victory,
Victory guaranteed by your mighty word.
It has already begun—
Who are they to challenge your authority?
No created being can contest you,
You are the Lord of Hosts.

Let all heaven and earth declare your glory
For you, O Lord, are subject to no one!
Let the fallen ones tremble
In fear of your return,
The battlefield awaits, O King of Kings,
It awaits your final victory, and peace restored.

Thank you, my dear King, for the freedom you give;
You offered freely of your own blood.
You did not die in vain—
Satan only thought he had won,
But you, Jesus, took all authority from him,
So that in your death we have life, freedom and victory.

Let all who stand in your way be struck down—
Crush them, O Lord, in your mighty hand.
Uproot this rebellion, O King,
For I see that you hate our sin;
Replace our wickedness
With the mighty works of your hands, lift us up!

continued

For you are Lord, God of heaven and earth,
You have created all things,
Power and majesty are yours alone!
Who can rebel against your laws?
Guide and direct your people, Lord,
Keep us from evil in these perilous days!

Give us courage, O Lord, to reject this rebellion.

A Single Tomorrow in a Land of Yesterdays

ESCAPE

As I perceive
The crushing tide of my reality,
I discern that it's too much for me.
Let me be!
Let me be!
Escape to my dream!

Now I see,
I see it, now, all too plainly—
The rising tide of my hostility.
Let me see,
Oh, let me see!
Escape to my dream!

So difficult for me,
This reality in which I seek.
The current too strong—it capsized me!
Set me free!
Set me free!
Escape to my dream!

Though it frightens me,
This truth I see,
It's so very simple: my fragility!
Let me be,
Please let me see!
Escape this dream!

The rise and fall of all I see
Batters my mind so treacherously.
Perception lost—it's gone from me;
Long twisted from my misery!
And I've seen it all so wrongly;
I've lost my touch with reality,
Help me, Lord, and set me free!   *continued*

A Single Tomorrow in a Land of Yesterdays

I await your hand so anxiously,
But all is spinning—washing away from me!
Dream versus Reality:
This war wages inside of me.
The waves rise steadily,
But what is that? What is that I see?
A mighty hand grabbing hold of me!

A Single Tomorrow in a Land of Yesterdays

THE FLAME

It all seems to fall upon me,
Brick by brick,
Stone by stone,
To crash down upon me.

All around it creeps closer,
Hour by hour,
Day by day,
To destroy me.

Darkness plunges down upon me,
Word by word,
Thought by thought,
To take my eyes from you.

Strengthen me, my Lord,
I cannot stand,
I'm breaking, dear God,
Pick me up, I pray.

These things would rob my joy,
Swing by swing,
Blow by blow,
Like a hammer they crush me.

Without warning I'm struck,
Weight by weight,
Load by load,
Heaped on to my defeat.

It longs to take my life,
Trial by trial,
Sin by sin,
To destroy my faith.

continued

A Single Tomorrow in a Land of Yesterdays

Lift me up, my Lord,
I'm falling,
I'm faint, my Savior,
Deliver me, I beg!

Pass me through the flame,
The Purifier's flame,
Cleanse from me
All impurities,
Pass me through the flame.
Restore my strength,
Give me wings to fly.
Restore my love —
Love for enemies,
Love for friends.
Great is the power of your love,
I yearn to love as you do.
Stand with me, my Lord,
Midst my pain,
My torment,
My weakness.
Thank you, King of heaven and earth
When all seems wrong,
You lift me up,
And pass me through the flame!

SWEET RELEASE

Before the altar I stand,
Carrying no sacrifice.
I struggle step by step,
Fighting my own desires—
Lust, sin, and wickedness—
All seeks to destroy!
I long to reach the top,
To lie down in sweet release,
Sacrifice me, Lord, I pray,
For I am the offering.
And my debt is already paid,
Yet I give myself to you.
Your resurrection is my life!
This life I live is not my own,
I give myself to you—
All doubt,
And disease,
And filth—
Every part of me
I release to you now!
Take it all, my Lord and Savior!
Kill all of me,
I am wretched and weak,
Restore my soul
With faithfulness,
And healing,
And cleansing—
I release myself to you,
Take every part of me, my Lord and Savior,
And make me a pure part of you!

FOR WHICH LIGHT IS NAMED

Many, many years we have wasted in darkness
What makes us such evil creatures?
Why do I cling to my own mind's darkness?
I stumble about in utter darkness,
Blind even to my own desires,
Answering to every evil whim of the surrounding black.
Why do we refuse the light?
What makes the dirt and dark so inviting?
I cannot see to find my way out,
Trapped by this darkness.
I thought it would keep me safe,
Safe from what, and from whom?
Safe from change and challenge and my hopeless desperations
But instead I have been chained—
Chained to my evil thoughts and desires,
To my wickedness and sins.
I need out, I need out!
Running frantically I find nothing can help,
Only in my despair do I cry out,
"Someone, anyone. Touch me, save me, help me, rescue me NOW!"
Out of the dark there shines a light,
A light like no other,
A light for which light is named;
It shines a perfect brilliance upon me,
And now I see
I was bound by my own darkness, my own chains;
The shackles that held me were of my own design,
My own malice had been my torment,
My own desires were my pitfalls.
But this light as I see it now,
It is my escape, my rescue.
Without it I cannot see the twisted thing, which I have become.

This new vision gives me strength,
For in the light there is an outstretched hand,
It is there only to save me.
But these chains—
I cannot break them, not with all my strength,
For I created them with my own strength,
And some other malice tightened them beyond my little power.
Only in my despair do I cry out,
"Lord, for you are my Lord, please, with your might
Would you save me from my sins?
For these awful things I have done
I am so very sorry,
And with my whole being I give myself to you.
I believe in you, I really believe in you;
So I ask you Lord to fill my life with your presence!"
Now His beautiful face is revealed to me
And His powerful voice I hear:
"My son, your faith has made you whole,
As I have created you to be.
Now live in my light and leave this terrible darkness.
Walk with me in freedom,
For your price was already paid.
So walk with me on the narrow path—
It is laid before you now,
Do not walk to either side of it,
Instead, stay by my side to sin no more"
My shackles simply fade away
As all power of imprisonment has vanished.
Even I begin to fade away,
My Lord replaces my weaknesses with His strengths.
With tears of joy I embrace my newly found King.
And step by step,
I walk with him in newness.
For my chains are broken—
I am bound no more.
My days are not always easy,
But with my eyes on Him, how can I fail?

MY AVENGER

Many enemies I have
Intending only to destroy
All you have graciously given me.
Your command,
Is to show them only love,
And what I do not understand is how?
My desire is to be yours,
A servant of the Most Holy,
And still they desire to do me harm!
I know, my Lord,
You have lifted me
Beyond all mortal reach,
But I beg you,
Forget not your word.
You have promised
That vengeance is yours,
And yours alone!
Who am I to stand in your way?
Let your wrath
Be poured out upon all evil!
Crush all wickedness!
Smite down all
Who have defiled your name!
For your name is Almighty God!
Keep my heart
From evil and malice,
And purify me, Dear Lord,
That your judgment
Would not fall my way.
I ask you, Lord,
To judge righteously
Those who have sought my destruction!
Hand out the penalty
For their sinful desires.
Whose wisdom compares to yours?

None in heaven,
Nor in earth
Can do as you have done,
And will do.
Time will come to pass
When all traces of evil
Are erased completely!
My heart desires vengeance,
Yet I know that it is yours,
Yours alone.
For that I rejoice!
For how can a sin-stained man
Judge man righteously?
I cannot,
Nor should I attempt to.
I was not meant to judge,
A corrupt man
Should not pass judgment.
So, my Lord and King,
I leave the Judgment to you,
Begging you, do not forget my case!
Forget not
The unlawful and unjust
Attacks of my enemies!
Forget not
Your promise,
And carry out what is yours,
And yours alone:
Vengeance!

HOW DARE YOU

You come to me
Bringing your temptation.
You come to me
Seeking my destruction.

This is my life
You seek to take.
This is my home
You seek to break.

Take another look,
My enemy.
Take another look,
There is more to see.
How dare you,
Come against me?
Go ahead and look
At who is with me!

You come to me
With your dirty rags.
You come to me
Bringing your plagues.

This is my life
You seek to take.
This is my home
You seek to break.

Take another look,
My enemy.
Take another look,
There is another with me!
How dare you,
Come against me?

A Single Tomorrow in a Land of Yesterdays

Go ahead and look,
God Almighty is with me!

You come to me
With disease and sickness.
You come to me
With evil and wickedness.

This is my life
You seek to take.
This is my home
You seek to break.

Get out of here,
My enemy!
Get out of here!
Go and flee!
You don't think I know
What you have done!
Let me tell you this:
I have already won!
Before me stands
God Almighty's only son!
You think that
You can come against me?
But you're forgetting
That I am free!

So, take another look,
My enemy.
Take another look,
There is another with me!
How dare you,
Come against me?
Go ahead and look,
Jesus Christ stands with me!

DEALINGS OF DEATH

Writhing pain of my withering existence,
Written in melancholy tones of stone and ash,
Beneath beaten boughs of no inheritance,
Thoughts and themes of fruitful future crash,
Crumbled scripts conceived by Death upon my crypt,
Mounds and mounds of murderous plots
Have warped with whispering wickedness my lips,
Gnarled with ghastly growths over my flowerpots.

Pulled with pronounced pain into Death's proximity,
Greatly grasping and groping for one hold on Life,
Holding the hand dealt while striding with insanity
Upon the muddied mound of meshing mirth and strife,
Whose headstone contains the stains of crimson blood,
Winded and weathered stone compelled by hands of bone
To bear and bring forth dismal death beneath the mud,
My melancholy mourning tones resound from stone to stone!

Desperately deceived by the dealings of Death,
His lies, like the swarming of flies, tied my mind,
Boundless butcheries blandly dealt with every breath,
Have certainly caused disease to make me blind,
Trepidations tripping the senses to seizing senselessness,
Brought back to better recollection in the bold, bright Sun of Truth,
Melting the melancholy tones of stone and ash to nothingness,
Away agonizing anticipation and behold the bright Sun of Truth!

Again the melancholy tones have groaned futility,
Failing to grasp the full function of the Sun of Truth,
Seizing the slipping opportunity to keep my sanity,
Peacefully pledged my meaning to the merciful Sun of Truth!

PRAISE

CHAMPION

It was You that named me,
You called me forth,
And claimed me.
"Champion" You called,
Champion I am,
No matter how small.
I have victory in You,
No loss I suffer,
Victory in all I say and do.
Day to day I live,
And win,
Because of the power you give.
I am not defeated,
Champion am I,
For You, the enemy has retreated.
It was You that named me,
You called me forth,
And claimed me.
"Champion" You called,
Champion I am,
No matter how small.
None can contest,
For You named me,
And with that name I am the best.
Many battles will I win,
Blessed by You,
Guaranteed victory to the very end.
It was You that named me,
You called me forth,
And claimed me.
"Champion" You called,
Champion I am,
No matter how small.

BY YOUR HAND

By your hand, the universe was formed,
Galaxy by galaxy,
Every star, you called forth by name
Every planet and moon.
By your hand, all things exist,
Everything came out of nothing.
You called forth earth,
With special purpose,
On it you placed life.
Creatures,
Plants,
And man.
Beauty was bestowed upon it,
Pointing back to you,
Our Creator,
Our Savior,
Our God and King.
By your hand, the mountains were called up,
Showing your majesty.
By your hand, the oceans were formed,
Showing the depths of your great love.
By your hand, plants and trees grew,
Telling of your wondrous provision.
By your hand, all creatures found life,
Telling of your power to create.
By your hand, the sunset was painted,
Pointing to you, the designer of all things.
All creation cries out,
"Holy, Holy, Holy is the Lord God Almighty"
This beauty, glorious and grand,
Marvelous in every way,
Is so insignificant
In comparison to what you have in store,
For those who are your children.
For by your hand, all heaven is paved in gold.

By your hand its peaks are pure ivory,
By your hand the Chosen finally rest—
In perfect peace
By your side for all eternity.
And all heaven and earth resound together, forever,
"Holy, Holy, Holy is the Lord God Almighty."

LORD OF GLORY

On the throne
Of power and authority
You are seated.
All things belong to you,
And all is in your kingdom.
All those who exalt themselves
Are shamed in your presence.
For you are
The Lord of Glory,
And all must kneel
At your throne,
And beg your mercy!
For all life
Proceeds from you,
And was called forth by you.
You named the beginning,
And you will name the end!
Before your throne,
All will stand
And pledge allegiance,
Or perish!
Too long,
Have we neglected
Your praise!
For you are
The Lord of Glory,
Worthy of all praise
Throughout all eternity.
Your name,
The greatest of all names,
Will be praised!

Splendor upon splendor,
And glory upon glory,
High above all else,
You are seated
Upon the Throne of Glory!
From the sound of your voice,
And the light from your eyes
Proceeds all power and authority!
For you are
The Lord of Glory,
All must kneel at your throne!

GLORIOUS

Let your praise dwell continuously on my lips,
Not merely a habit;
Not done for repetition's sake,
But truly, and sincerely, an effort
Of all my being,
To bring glory to the Most Glorious Name of all!

For in your praise I find my reason for taking breath,
Now and forever.
For beyond all hope, above all fear and dread,
You have delivered me from certain doom!
Now with my whole heart, and my hands raised,
I give glory to the One who has all Glory!

Let my mind forever dwell upon you,
Not only my thoughts,
But the very essence of all I am!
Let my life be lived
As a sign at the crossroads —
Directing all to the Most Glorious Path!

Let the earth forever sing your praise:
Land and sky and sea!
Let the firmament lift its arms,
Forever praising, humbly at your feet.
Let all creation fear the Holy One,
And sing glory to the Most Glorious Name of all!

PRAISES

All the host of heaven sings your praise,
All creation shouts your glory,
For you alone are God,
The King seated upon the throne of majesty,
Power is in your hands,
All things have life through your breath!

Let the rocks cry out,
Let the people sing,
"Glory to the King of Kings,"
All earth sings praise,
Your children's hands are raised!

The vast universe cries your name,
All creation shouts your glory,
It is you who is worthy,
The King seated upon the highest mountain,
All hosts at your command,
All creation breathes your breath of life!

Let the people cry out,
Let the mountains sing,
"Glory to the King of Kings,"
All earth resounds the praise,
Your children's hands are raised!

The heavenly choir sings glory to your name,
All life offers thanks to you,
For you are the giver of life,
The King of Power and Majesty,
The angels bask in your glory,
And all creation shouts your praise!

continued

Let the earth resound,
Let the people sing,
"Glory to the King of Kings,"
Heaven and earth in unison praise,
All your people's hands are raised,
Mountains bow at your feet,
You are King on the mercy seat,
Full of power, majesty and glory,
None compare to your story,
Let all creation sound,
Let all people sing,
"Glory to the King of Kings!"

SUFFICIENT

Should my life span a thousand million years,
And with every breath I thanked you,
All my gratitude would fall deadly short of sufficient.
Though I should spend every coin of my treasure hoard,
And try with undying devotion to repay you,
All the gold, of all the world, would fall deadly short of sufficient.
Although I should spend my entire life in service,
Offering myself as your unworthy slave,
Surrendering my all to you, still, would fall deadly short
of sufficient
Even though I should sacrifice all that I have, and more,
Giving to you all that I have ever had, and ever dreamed of,
All this is yet deadly short of sufficient!
Though I give to you every word written,
Every hope hoped, and every wage earned,
I still remain short, inadequate, and utterly insufficient!

Yet you care beyond all cares,
You love beyond all loves,
You bless beyond all blessings,
And you forgive beyond all forgiveness!

I am made your son,
Even though I stand before you
Ashamed of my life,
In the realization that by your great mercies
I need not be sufficient because you are sufficient—
Beyond all my insufficiencies!

IF I COULD PAINT LIKE YOU

I watch the sunset,
In awe of the splendor,
The beauty you create.
As you hold this spinning world in your hand.
The picture you make is so beautiful
No artist can even begin to copy it.
I see no brush strokes,
It is on no canvas.
The skill of your hands is immeasurable,
Man tries and tries to create like you,
All the while he forgets,
He also is created —
As a lesser reflection of you.
In his heart he desires your greatness,
His mind thinks,
"If I could paint like you.
Maybe I would be great,
Maybe then I would be powerful,
Ridding myself of you."
I watch as the stars appear slowly
In this living, moving picture.
I think of how you hold this universe
This vast, mighty universe,
In the palm of your hand.
Yet you see me,
Just a tiny, tiny speck of paint
On this world we call Earth.
You hear my every cry,
And you desire to dwell in my heart.
I see now this picture you paint,
The universe,
The stars,
The planets,
The moon and earth and everything in them.

All these things are painted with the most beautiful paint,
A paint that man cannot attempt to create,
This paint is your love.
Man's only way to greatness,
Is to give up his search,
And to humble himself at your feet, Almighty God,
For you are the Painter, the Creator, and the Possessor
Of heaven and earth and everything in them!

ETERNAL

You were there before the beginning,
The beginning guided by your mighty hand,
The planets: named and set in motion by your word,
Your breath gave all creation life,
You were there in creation; you were there at the fall of man,
The Earth was flooded by your right hand, and all the world wept,
You began again, and called your people forth,
Beginning with Abraham,
They were a mighty nation, with your blessing and power,
The weak were made strong and they flourished by your name,
You called them forth from slavery,
Sending a deliverer named Moses,
You set them free, and sent them in search of
Your Promised Holy Land,
You delivered the land to them with Joshua as their leader,
They conquered and claimed for your name,
Your people grew great, and you called judges to help
them in need,
Your hand guided Samson as he slew a thousand Philistines,
You were there when David came to be king —
A man after your own heart —
And as David passed his power to his son, Solomon the Wise,
You sent fire to answer prayers at the temple,
Looking down, you saw it destroyed
As your people withdrew from your will,
Then you called them back to the Promised Land,
By your hand they came and rebuilt the temple,
And their city, Jerusalem,
The prophets came under your power and spoke of a Savior,
They prophesied of the coming Messiah, though none knew when,
And few knew Him when He came to earth as a normal man,
When He came many were deceived, and He was rejected,
Your spiritual leaders rejected Him as one doomed to die,
And die He did, for all the sinners, of all the earth, for all time,

Yet that was not the end, for the Savior not only died,
but rose again
To proclaim freedom to all that believe,
Your word speaks of all the wonders He, and His disciples, did,
Many died for His name including: Peter, and Paul,
But to them, and all others that believe,
You give the ultimate gift: Eternal life!
And you are, and were, there before the beginning,
And after the end of time,
For you are Eternal; you have always been, and always will be,
Almighty God!

PROVIDER

Your provision is miraculous—
Daily feeding and clothing your children,
Innumerable they are,
Yet you provide abundantly;
Extraordinarily you bless all.
Times without
Are few,
And far between.
You hear and answer all cries,
Life is a struggle,
Impossible to obtain without you,
All things come by
And through you!
Many come and ask,
Unworthy they are—
All of them—
Yet you hear and answer,
Rewarding for belief and faith!
You are the provider,
Providing all heaven and earth,
Graciously do you bestow gifts,
Selfishly we grab,
Ungrateful for the many provisions,
Yet you continuously give,
Never to be repaid,
Out of your immeasurable Love!
We owe you all thanks,
And all faithfulness!
So I stand resolutely and cry,
"Thank you, God and Father, my Lord,
And my precious Savior,
Thank you for your provision!
Your provision,
For which I am unworthy!

Thank You,
Forever and ever,
Without end,
Thank You!"

A Single Tomorrow in a Land of Yesterdays

MY HANDS

From your high place of discernment,
You've perceived my every deed,
And searched my every motive.
Since we first met,
And my life became yours,
I've set my heart and soul to worship you—
Without instruction
My hands followed where my heart has ever led!

Let it be known, let it be seen,
That my tired hands
Shall ne'er tire in praising my King!

May my soul rejoice,
And my strings proclaim in symphony,
The wonders of knowing you!
For you are the inspiration of my song,
And what causes my voice to sing.
Remember every strike of the string,
Every key that I play,
For long ago I gave it all to you,
Seeking no glory in it,
For glory and majesty are yours alone!

Let it be known, let it be seen,
That my tired hands
Shall ne'er tire in praising my King!

My life, plain and unadorned,
Is, and shall be, spent in your service—
Every thread I've held, every stitch sewn,
With greater good in mind,
That with remembrance of me
My offspring should always be reminded
For whom my life is ever lived.

A Single Tomorrow in a Land of Yesterdays

For long ago I gave it all to you,
Seeking no glory in it,
For glory and majesty are yours alone!

Let it be known, let it be seen,
That my tired hands
Shall ne'er tire in praising my King!

THE ONE OF ABUNDANT WORTH

I lift my praise to you,
As my song I raise to you,
I praise you with my mouth,
As this time I take out
To Praise the One of Abundant Worth,
To sing your glory with all my words!
I give glory to all you do,
You are Holy and you are true.
All your children sing,
"Glory to you, my King",
To you who are worthy without end,
I lift my outstretched hands, again.
To Praise the One of Abundant Worth,
To sing your glory with all my words!
My life was nothing before you came,
I lifted my hands and called your name,
To you I gave my soul, unclean,
And you gave a new beginning,
My life belongs to you,
Glory to the One who is true,
I lift my praise to you,
As my song I raise to you,
I Praise the One of Abundant Worth,
I sing your glory with all my words!

MASTER

Autumn leaves,
Brilliantly hued
By your master hand,
Shades of red,
Yellow,
Orange, and bronze.
You are the Master,
The Creator,
The Possessor of beauty.
All around are glimpses
Of power,
Of care and love,
All hands point to heaven,
Where you reside in glory,
From mountain peak,
To valley deep,
From river rushing,
To the silent lake,
Glade,
And field.
You are the Master,
The Creator,
The Possessor of beauty.
In spring you bring new life,
Summer pinnacles that life,
And all are busy caring for your world.
Autumn colors signify
The passing of summer's abundant life,
Warning of the coming cold,
And all colors washed clean
By Winter's gleaming snow.
You alone bring,
And take,
Life.

continued

All life owes itself to you,
For you are the Master,
The Creator,
The Possessor of all life, and all beauty!

MY THANKS

My thanks will not suffice.
For me you paid the price,
You died and rose again,
I'm freed from my burden.

My thanks will not do
So I give my life to you,
I don't have much to give,
But for you I desire to live.

My thanks is too small
For me you gave your all,
You gave the ultimate gift,
In praise, my hands I lift.

My thanks will not cover
My sins undiscovered,
I only beg forgiveness,
For my lustful wickedness.

My thanks will never pay
So, on this altar, my sins I lay,
Take from me all you see
That steals from me the victory.

My thanks I give to you
Even though it will not do,
I give my time 'til my last breath
For you I'll live until my death.

My thanks I lay down
'Til I receive my crown,
Thank you, Lord, for all you've done
Thank you, for making me your son.

THE TEST

Very few things
Stand the test of time,
Yet you,
All things about you,
Have already spanned
An eternity.
You are ageless,
And ancient,
Speaking wisdom unattainable
By mortal man.
Your very word
Spoken in every culture,
Written in every tongue,
Desired by all,
Has stood
Undeniable and uncontestable
Above all challengers.
Love, sacrifice, salvation,
Spoken from your tongue,
Translated by men,
Acted upon
By your own offspring.
You have stood the test of time,
Crushing all who
Would seek to remove you
From your seat of victory,
Judging all,
Knowing all,
Loving all,
You desire only
Salvation for all who seek!

For it is you,
You alone,
Who can stand through all time,
And all eternity
As King of Kings,
And Lord of Lords,
God of all ages,
And Lord of all people!

MY GOD AND KING

My God and King,
Your Spirit frees my heart to sing
I was a slave, bound in pain,
You freed me from my chains.
Because of you I have no sin,
I can lift my voice again.

My Savior and Friend,
You saved me from a dreadful end.
I was on the road of Death and Shame
'Til you pardoned my blame.
You were bruised, broken for me,
And through your blood I am free.

My Lord and Peace,
Your power sets my heart at ease.
My life is in you,
Everything I do, I do in you.
By your word I make my way;
Without you there is no day.

My Lord and Light,
Your presence gives me sight.
In your word is my path,
Without your Spirit I would not last.
You bring me hope, peace and love,
Showering down from your throne above.

My God and King,
Have mercy on this soul I bring.
I am sorry I so often fall,
Please, Lord, lift me above it all.
Set me on solid ground,
Call your angels to gather 'round.

A Single Tomorrow in a Land of Yesterdays

My Savior and Friend,
I beg you: stay with me to the end.
No matter what happens along the way,
Strengthen me, Lord, I pray.
I love you, Lord, with my whole heart,
From your path I will not depart.

My Lord, and King,
In your presence forever we'll sing.

IN AWE

I come before your throne,
A slave I should be,
Yet a child I am made.
A lowly man am I,
Yet you look upon me smiling.
I lie at your Holy feet
Seeking mercy and help,
With pity in your eyes
You lift me up!
I do not comprehend —
I am filled with weakness,
And sin.
The very thing you hate
I am covered in!
I am in awe of your vast mercies!
Smile never fading,
You watch my daily failures.
In you resides only love,
In that infinite love
Stands my salvation!
My life is in you,
My peace is in you,
Without you I am nothing,
You are my everything!
I do not understand —
I am filled with weakness,
And sin.
The very thing you hate,
I am covered in!
I am in awe of your powerful presence!
In your wonderful light,
My darkness flees in terror!
And at your feet
I am as you created me to be,
Washed by your own blood.

I am spotless,
Free of sin,
Free of weakness,
Free to be a child of the Most Holy!
I am in awe of you,
I will praise your name forever!

THANK YOU

For all things, I say thank you,
Your power and presence and truth.
For all things great and small
You are exalted as Lord of all.

Thank you, so much
For your Spirit's gentle touch.
For the life you alone can give
In your spirit we now live.

Thank you, for the blood you shed,
I know it was for me you bled.
Thank you, for the victory
By your blood I am set free.

Thank you, for the world you made
The mountain, forest, and glade.
The plants and animals and sky above
Are nothing without your great love.

Thank you, Lord, for abundant life
So I can live without the strife.
Thank you, for rescuing me
From my sins I've been made free.

CHRISTIAN LIFE

YOUR WAY

As I travel this dusty road, that you call my life,
I find the more I struggle to find my own way
The more I find no path at all,
Only pain and struggle,
Isolation and desolation.
So Lord, I lift my hands to you,
Pleading with you,
"Give me the wings to fly away."

As my road climbs ever steeper, you call it a trial,
I find that in you are the only answers I desire.
I find my way in you,
You lift me up, O Lord,
Higher than I could ever imagine,
So Lord, I lift my hands to you,
Begging You,
"Bring me close enough to see your face."

As I find myself on this mountain peak, I feel your embrace,
But in my heart I wonder why you have not shown the way.
Speak to me, Lord of Lords,
To hear your voice is to know the way,
Help me, my King,
To silence my own voice,
So Lord, I lift my hands to you,
"Please, my Lord and King, reveal this hidden path for me."

As I await your answer I hear no voice, but I know your
presence—
I am anxious to know the way; loud and clear you say
"The way is here before you.
Do not think in terms of your power,
But in mine."

continued

It is so clear before me now
So Lord, I lift my hands to you,
"Thanking you for the wings you gave me as I fly your way."

A Single Tomorrow in a Land of Yesterdays

FREEDOM REIGN, FREEDOM RING

The things I see—seldom thought,
Soaring upon revelation,
The freedom—bloodshed bought,
Nation conquers nation.

Fields spoiled with young blood,
Hero and coward side by side
Falling breathless in the mud,
Sacrificed lives for nation's pride.

Duty calling to memory
Selfless deeds—rightful honor,
Left not to fields of glory,
Etched forever and kept in store.

Forget not fallen heroes,
Nor the cause of freedom,
Nor its defeated lows,
Nor the bloodshed ransom.

Freedom reigns in the blood,
Ringing still upon the field,
Left to rot in the mud
By those who to evil yield.

Remember still the price paid;
That the power of justice
And the tyranny some victor's made
Was caused by men just like us.

The cause of freedom in the end—
High banners of the just
Caught by Heaven's wind,
Cannot be allowed to suffer rust.

continued

A Single Tomorrow in a Land of Yesterdays

An evil day it would be
To lay down freedom's cause—
Leaving captive to captivity,
In the bite of oppressor's jaws.

Let the free to the captive bring,
Even blood shed in the fight—
Freedom reign, freedom ring—
The just will see the cause is right!

NEVER

Though my Enemy stands over me,
Bloody mace in upraised hand,
Death to my body is my victory,
For him I will never, never stand!

Though he take my very life,
Mercilessly gloating over the fallen,
Ever filling the land with strife,
My service of him will never, ever begin.

My enemy maliciously smiling,
Ready to strike my deathblow,
His face and eyes menacingly seething,
Fingers gripping his mace, never will he let go.

Though my Enemy stands over me,
Bloody mace in upraised hand,
Death to my body is my victory,
For him I will never, never stand!

Though he stand over me,
Wanting only my destruction,
I hold something he does not see,
It is my hope and my salvation.

Though death be all around,
And I myself, about to slip away,
My blood may drip to the ground,
But I will never, never walk his way!

Though my Enemy stands over me,
Bloody mace in upraised hand,
Death to my body is my victory,
For him I will never, never stand!

continued

Though his deathblow fall my way,
And his mace comes down forcefully,
His malicious smile will soon fade away,
For I am given the victory!

Though I am few inches from death,
My salvation is the form of a mighty sword,
By God's word, and provision, I am blessed:
By the Word my Enemy is gored.

By the sword, my Enemy is struck,
By the sword, my Enemy gives up!

Though my Enemy stands over me,
Bloody mace in upraised hand,
Death to my body is my victory,
For him I will never, never stand!

COME BACK!

Come back to the Lord, my people,
Come back! Come back!
To the place we met Him,
And cast away all sin—
To the place of our redemption,
To the Maker of our Salvation!

Come back to the Lord, my people,
Come back! Come back!
Difficult it seems
To fight the enemy;
Yet our victory
Is already guaranteed!

Come back to the Lord, my people,
Come back! Come back!
To our Savior, and friend,
Before the end;
To be forgiven,
For all have sinned!

Come back to the Lord, my people,
Come back! Come back!
Ask him now to save your soul,
He'll give new life, and make you whole,
He'll take your trouble,
And wash you white as snow!

THE KING'S ARMOR

As a warrior of old I go forth,
But my battle is not with the body of man,
Nor do I wage war that blood might be spilled,
For my battle is against the evil and rebellious spirit,
I fight even myself in this ageless war of Spirit
divided against Flesh,
All mankind has entered this very same war,
And all fight for the good, or the bad,
I go into battle with the knowledge:
One day good will win the final battle
And the war!
I do not go unprepared,
For my King has prepared a suit of indestructible armor,
And with that, I go forward to fight, shining with His glory,
So that all evil flees the very sight of my sword,
My sword contains the very spirit of Him that sent me,
He has graven into it words that I should never forget,
And those same words strike fear into the hearts of the enemy
As they shine like the stars in the heavens,
And strike down all that would stand in the way of their purpose!
This armor I wield, made by the King Himself, is glorious,
It is dreadful to the evil, filling all foes with terror of its might,
Yet the faithful are filled with courage because of it,
About my waist is the Belt of His Truth,
It shines a lovely light before me, and displaces all hint
of darkness,
Above the Belt shines forth the Breastplate of His righteousness,
Keeping away the wounds of wickedness from my heart,
Around my feet is readiness for battle,
Readiness, which comes from knowing the news of His Peace,
To finish the gifts of the King is the Helmet of His Salvation,
That I might call upon him in times of dire need
To be delivered from the arms of my enemies!
And so that I might not be struck down in this war against evil
I carry also the Shield of Faith!

A Single Tomorrow in a Land of Yesterdays

No foe can stand against me!
No enemy may come against the forces of the King
and be victorious!
And no retreat will ever be sounded, unless we all perish,
For there is no armor guarding our backs,
And all who flee will surely be slain,
But take no heed to retreat!
For surely, all foes are defeated by us,
The faithful!
And no gates can possibly stand before us,
The servants, and warriors, of the King of Kings
And the Lord of Lords!

NOTHING

Along the roadside sits a man,
He holds a sign and a can.
Years of pain carved in his face,
To his family, a drunken disgrace.

"How did he end up this way?"
I hear their voices say.
His eyes bear years of rejection,
All this man needs is your redemption.

And I offer him nothing,
Not even a prayer of blessing.
I choose to turn a blind eye,
And in heaven I hear you cry.

You have given me so much,
And in return I choose not to touch
Those who are rejected by men,
Take from me, dear Lord, this awful sin.

Your love, I do not show
To those I perceive too low.
His pain is nothing to me,
And I claim, "You've set me free."

And I give him nothing,
Not even a word of comforting.
"Lord, send someone his way,"
Is all I can find to pray.

Lord, break my cold heart of stone,
Break me, Lord, to the very bone.
I am as blind as I can be,
Please open my eyes so I can see.

A Single Tomorrow in a Land of Yesterdays

Make me to love as you do,
Loving all, faithful and true.
All are your children,
Even the sick and broken.

A Single Tomorrow in a Land of Yesterdays

MY NATION, MY PEOPLE

Awake, my nation,
And arise from your slumber.
You were formed by God's command,
His laws were made your laws,
His name printed on your books and money,
You say, "In God we trust",
Yet you have forsaken His ways.

Come back, my people,
And throw down your walls of ignorance,
Come back to the One who formed you!
You were created for freedom of religion,
Not for freedom from the Truth,
For there is one Truth, and only one Way,
All others lead to certain destruction.

Rise up, my nation,
God cannot be taken forcefully from what He made,
If you abandon God,
Then you forsake what united us from the beginning!
You should ask Him for guidance,
Not separate Him from our legislation,
Do not doom us all by your stupidity!

Awake, my people,
From your sleep, and open your blind eyes,
The Truth will make Himself known!
Step from the darkness with open eyes,
And you will see our elected leaders
Have taken us far astray,
Come back to Him that made us, to Him that can save us!

Unite us again, O Lord,
In common worship of your Holy Name,
For you called us to your side,
And we abandoned your guidance for our own.
Call us again, dear Lord,
Call us again to your side, and claim us as your own,
Without you we have become nothing.

Redeem us, Lord, I pray!

SHALL NEVER YIELD

When I stand in place I am torn in two,
So now, as I go forward I ask You,
"Which way from here, my Lord?
And when can I lay aside this sword?"
My enemies are many and great,
It seems I have asked for help too late.
"How do I make it through?
How do I, at the end, stay true?"
When all rush in for my defeat—
Even the rocks beneath my feet!
You asked me why I lingered there,
But my every turn seems to lead nowhere.
Don't let indecision be the end of me;
Send the Guiding Light that I may see.
When all paths look bleak and perilous
Give me strength; make me courageous!
When my enemy's encampment surrounds
Give me strength to boldly stand my ground!
When my enemy's banner is brought high to taunt me
Let him know that he will never daunt me!
And though I stand alone upon the battlefield,
Unto him I shall never yield;
For it is your sword that I wield,
And it contains a power uncontainable—
The fear in my enemy is truly undeniable!
No force of man, beast, or spirit
May from my hand steal it—
For though my enemies are many and great,
My Help has not come too late!
I have always carried it in my hand;
It burns brighter than the sun-scorched sand!
For the weapon you have given me
Is truly mighty indeed!

NO EXCUSE

I have no excuse, my Lord, my King,
For why to my sins I cling
Since you hanged on a tree for me
That from those sins I should be free

I have no excuse, my Lord, my King,
Why for you I do not sing
You took my sins to Calvary
So they might have no power over me

I have no excuse, my King and Lord,
Why for you I do not take up the sword
You bled and died for me to save
So I no longer should stay a slave

I have no excuse, my Lord, my King,
Why to you no souls I bring
Your spirit empowers me from above
Why do I live as if I have no love?

I have no excuse, my Lord and Friend,
Why I live as if I will not end
You have told me you would come again
Why do I continue in my horrible sin?

I have no excuse, my Lord and Savior,
Why for you I do not labor
You Son was bruised and broken for me
Yet I live as though you've done nothing for me

So I ask you, my Lord, my King,
To give a voice with which to sing
Of how you bled and died for me
And how you've set me free

continued

So I ask you, my Lord, my King,
To give me your sword to swing
That I might fight the world of sin
And bring your life to them again

So I ask you, my Lord, my King,
Help me my friends to bring
To your altar to set them free
So together we'll live eternally

RENEWAL

DEEPEN ME

Deepen me
As rains upon the open sea.
Reveal to me the great depths—
Awesome power behind the precepts!
Let my life decrease
As your will I seize.
Let power fall
Upon my life, so small.

Deepen me
Take me to heights I've never seen.
Bring close your spirit;
Speak that I might hear it!
Enlarge your life in me;
Reveal what I cannot see!
You reign as King forever,
Praise of your name cease never!

Deepen me
As snow upon the highest peak.
May my life bear your mark
In this journey through the lonely dark!
Spring forth in my soul,
And make me completely whole.
Your design is my desire—
My Savior, my heart's fire!

THE SUN

In the west, dark clouds arise—
"Here comes the storm,"
Proclaims the fury of the wind,
And ever watchful stands the Sun above.
"Your wrath brings no fury that I cannot brighten!"
Dark clouds lined with the Sun's gold and silver
Reach forth in desperation;
Grip only loosened for a short while—
Above the storm's rage shines the undaunted Sun
Ever weakening the cloud's rebellion.
While the storm rises, and fades, the Sun remains ever constant:
Unchallenged and unafraid!
And even as the darkness passes
His strength is revealed in His glorious light,
The storm brought thunder, lightning, and fierce winds,
But in his inevitable end he was broken, and shamed,
By the presence of the Sun's splendor,
A beauty unexpected and unlooked for—
The majestic form of a rainbow!
With glory unfurled,
The Sun shines ever on!
"Look for me, my precious lands,
For I shine despite the storm!
Through the storm and clouds of Darkness
I have ever shone and will ever shine!
Forget me not when the trouble comes—
I am the Light of the world, forever and always!"
In the west, dark clouds arise—
"Here comes the storm,"
Proclaims the fury of the wind,
And ever watchful stands the Sun above.
"Your wrath brings no fury that I cannot brighten!"

A Single Tomorrow in a Land of Yesterdays

HERE

Often I wonder
Why I struggle with so much,
And for so long,
Only to come here.
Progress seems so minute,
Victory has escaped me.
All is lost
To despair and anguish.
My demise,
My only companion;
Without hope I fight on.
Long have I sought
For peace,
And long has it fled.
Weaknesses plague
And mistakes ensnare.
Surrender
Is my only hope for freedom.
To possess much
Is to be possessed by much.
Giving all away
Brings peace and life.
I see now
Why I have come here.
With purpose you brought me here:
To rely on you!
For in you is all I seek.
You gently call,
"Come here. Come here, to me."
Here and now
All I thought I had,
Is gone.
And in you,
All needs are fulfilled.

MY PLEDGE

Many years have I wasted,
But no more;
I pledge myself to you.

May my life please you;
More than me, me in you.
You are my only way,
No more waste, or delay.
My soul needs cleansed,
Bathed in your blood, and rinsed.

Many years have I wasted,
But no more;
I pledge myself to you.

Make in me something new,
Something holy, like you.
You are what I need,
I give you my creed:
From you I will not fall,
For you are Lord of all.

Many years have I wasted,
But no more;
I pledge myself to you.

Today, I pledge to you:
I will honor you.
My heart is in your hand,
My life at your command.
I will do what you say,
That is my pledge, today!

A Single Tomorrow in a Land of Yesterdays

THE ATTACK

That fateful day,
Forever remembered—
Great was our loss,
Not only in lives,
But in freedom.
Our fragile security
Was crushed.
Our strength seemed
Just another victim.
The cowards brought
Fear and terror.
No longer did we
Triumph in the deeds of man.
The attack brings
Reality too close.
For man's deeds,
Are shameful and evil.
In the towers,
Man exalts himself,
And in the attack,
Man also exalts himself.
Let us turn our eyes to Heaven!
Let us exalt
Him who is worthy!
Let us turn our eyes to Heaven,
Where God cries out,
"Come to me,
I will lift you above this.
Out of reach
Of all attacks.

continued

Only I can rescue you,
So turn your hearts to me.
Repent and be saved.
For in me are
Peace and security,
That none can take away!"

FORTRESS

My life seems like a mountain range,
My spirit rises and falls
With every peak and valley.
The longer I live
The more valleys I discover.
Emotions twist and cover my path,
Hiding the plateau I seek.
Atop the mountain, I feel I could fly,
And in the valleys
I lose my will to continue.
Where is that which holds steadfast
Through all peaks and valleys?
My God built a fortress
Upon a high plateau of solid rock.
There is my refuge
To hold fast through life's storm.
I seek this fortress,
And its high tower,
With all that is in me.
I must focus,
Not on my problems,
But on my path.
The mist that covers my eyes,
Though it interferes,
Through it my path leads
To the very gates of refuge.
There will I dwell
With my God and King;
Never returning to the valley below!

I PRAY

Lord, show me the way
As I begin my day.
Show me your spirit;
Speak, so I might hear it.
Lord, invade my life
And take all my strife.

Lift me up, I pray,
And fly me away!
Keep me strong,
That I might carry on.
Shield me, Lord,
From the enemy's sword!

I long to see you when
All evil is forever broken.
You will triumph then
Over death, darkness, and sin.
A day of days that will be
When you have final victory!

Lift me up, I pray
And keep me strong today.
Help me to carry on,
For my journey is long.
Shield me, Lord,
From the enemy's sword!
Lord, show me your way,
As I begin my day.
Stand by me, Lord, I pray.

A Single Tomorrow in a Land of Yesterdays

ARROGANCE WILL PASS

Strike down the arrogant, O Lord,
Those who exalt themselves above you,
They laugh at you, and mock your word!
Their lives are in your hands,
Yet they shake their fists at heaven,
You love them beyond all curses,
And still they blaspheme your holy name!
The name above all names,
And they take it in vain,
Through the mud they drag your name,
And the name of your faithful!
Who are they to stand in the presence of Almighty?
And make wicked jokes?
They are disrespectful,
Deserving no pity!
Crush the arrogant, O Lord,
Crush them in the palm of your mighty hand,
They laugh at you, and mock your word!
The call themselves "mighty",
They are no mightier than ants,
Yet they put themselves before you!
They are deceived, Lord,
For there is none who can come before you,
None who can call themselves "righteous",
For you alone are righteous and holy,
You alone are mighty and powerful!
Open the eyes of the arrogant, O Lord,
For their day will soon pass,
They have been deceived,
And when that day comes they will stand naked before you!

continued

No longer will they mock, making jest of your name,
For they will see all your glory
And tremble in your presence,
Their knees will be forced down, bowing before you,
For you are Almighty God,
And none can stand before you,
Not a single one!
All pretenses will pass away,
There will be none deceived in your holy presence,
In the presence of Almighty all eyes will be open to His glory!
And if the arrogant come before Him,
Still neglecting His due praise,
They will be crushed,
Struck down by the hand of Almighty God!

SOMETHING HOLY

Begin in me something holy,
Make my heart to shine
As polished silver,
Proclaiming
For all to hear:
"You are holy,
In the holiest of ways!"
Begin in me something mighty,
Make my mouth to speak
Like tongues of fire,
Proclaiming
For all to hear:
"You are mighty,
The mightiest of all!"
Begin in me something holy,
Make my life to shine,
As Your glory
I proclaim
For all to hear:
"Forever you are holy,
In the holiest of ways!"
Begin in me something righteous,
Make my life
To reflect you,
As I proclaim
For all to hear:
"You are righteous,
You alone are righteous!"
Begin in me something holy,
Make me to shine.
As I carry your light
I proclaim,
For all to hear:
"You are Holy,
In the Holy of Holies!"

RENEW

Renew in me all I need
To overcome my selfish greed,
Show me all that pleases you,
Renew my strength to get me through.

Let your blood cover my sins of old,
Soften my heart, my heart so cold,
Break down the walls I have built,
And take from me my abundant guilt.
These things I have, I do not need,
Take them, Lord! Take them, I plead!

Renew in me all I need
To overcome my selfish greed,
Show me all that pleases you,
Renew my strength to get me through.

This greed, which drives my soul to sin,
Remove it, dear Lord, so I may start again!
These walls that I have built in haste,
Crush them, and leave them in waste.
These things I have, I do not need,
Take them, Lord! Take them, I plead!

Renew in me all I need
To overcome my selfish greed,
Show me all that pleases you,
Renew my strength to get me through.

In you I have all I need,
You removed my walls and my greed!
My life is renewed by you,
You give strength; you make me true!
Without you I am not living,
You bless me, Lord! You keep on giving!

A Single Tomorrow in a Land of Yesterdays

I am lifted,
I rejoice in you!
I am refreshed, renewed!

OF LOVE, PEACE, AND JOY

Man often wanders,
Seeking,
Never finding.
Many times have I sought,
And failed to find
That which brings
Love, peace, and joy.
Universally are they sought,
And universally
They do elude capture.
They do not flee.
Only do we seek
In the wrong places.
Ages of men have passed,
And ages of men
Have sought
That which brings
Love, peace, and joy.
I say,
To all who hear,
In you are they found!
In you
Lies all I have searched for.
In you
Are my love, peace, and joy.
Pages and pages
Of history are written,
And your Name is on every one,
As author!
Why can't we see?
I speak of a search,
Yet there is no search.

For it is plain to see
You are the source,
That which brings
Love, peace, and joy!

CLOSER

Closer: where I need to be,
Closer to you,
And farther from me.

Draw me closer to you,
Far from my flesh,
In you is truth
That I seek without rest.
I belong in you
Not in this Earth,
Evil and untrue,
Deceiving my spiritual birth.

Closer: where I need to be,
Closer to you,
And farther from me.

Pull me to your side,
Away from sin,
For you are my pride,
And with you I begin.
You bring new life
To my wretched flesh;
Taking away strife,
In you I am blessed!

Closer: where I need to be,
Closer to you,
And farther from me.

Standing in your presence
Though I am unworthy;
I bow beneath your brilliance
In the Kingdom built for me.

My flesh is passed away,
And I am whole again,
No longer to go astray,
Finally free of sin's oppression!

Closer: where I need to be,
Closer to you,
And farther from me.

FORMED ANEW

Form me as the crashing sea
Forms the crags of the coastal waters,
Just as the waves pound the stubborn rock
So pound my soul and shape it anew.
Just as the stone is ground to dust,
And every particle is swept to sea, and forgotten,
So is my soul ground, and my sin
Swept into the Sea of Forgetfulness!

Shape me as the relentless wind
Shapes the mountaintops,
Just as the wind beats the stubborn rock
So beat my soul and form it anew.
Just as soil and stone are broken down,
And every piece carried far, and forgotten,
So does the Renewing Wind of your Spirit
Carry my sins as far as east is from west!

Mold me as the ever-dripping water
Molds the underground rock formations,
Just as drops perpetually caress the stubborn rock
So caress my soul and form it anew.
Just as persistence and long-suffering are shaped in stone,
And every remnant of ugliness is washed and forgotten,
So also you cleanse me and make me beautiful,
And I am broken, a stubborn rock, and formed anew!

HEAVEN

EVERLASTING PARADISE

I long to see the crown you give,
To walk heaven's streets freely,
I long to live the life you lived,
To love all sincerely.

Help me, Lord, to find the way,
Help me, Lord, to find out how,
To live a holy life today,
Living the Life you allow.

One day I will sing forever,
One day I will walk on polished gold,
I will praise your always—forever.
You take away fear and doubt, hot and cold!

Since my sins are forgiven,
And I have found new life,
I will walk with you in heaven,
In everlasting paradise!

Thank You, Lord, for all you've done,
I look forward to your soon-coming return,
I will scan the clouds looking for the Son,
Save my loved ones; please, don't let them burn!

Bring all to you that do not know
Of the endless love you give,
Free them, Lord, let them show
All the people the life you lived!

Heaven is His gift
For all, you see.
Abandon the life you lived!
Receive the gift; receive it freely!

continued

Since my sins are forgiven,
And I have found new life,
I will walk with you in heaven
In everlasting paradise!

A Single Tomorrow in a Land of Yesterdays

FIND HIM

With Him by my side
For in Him I reside,
My life has been blessed,
As many have guessed,
Why am I so happy?
Well, my Lord set me free,
And with that freedom,
I live in His kingdom,
He loves me eternally,
And answers my every plea,
I long that you would find Him too,
Beyond death He'll carry you through!
Forever we'll be His children,
And together rejoice in heaven!

THEY MUST KNOW

They must know what you have done,
You came from heaven—God's only son.
You bled and died in terrible pain
To break the grip of sin's chains.

They must see who you really are
You must open their eyes and reveal your scars.
Help them, Lord, to see their own prison
And show to them you truly are risen.

They must know the pain that sins cause,
And without you that all is lost.
For you created this world we live in
I am sorry, Lord; we filled it with sin.

They must know how our sins hurt you
Make them see—in you lives the only Truth.
For you, Jesus, gave us the way out,
So that in you there is no doubt.

They must know what will become of us
If in you we have no trust.
You are what we always look for
We must have faith to open our hearts' door.

They must see where we will be
When our hearts are yours, we will be free.
Free from all that binds us here,
I know in heaven all will be perfectly clear.

They must know the gift you give
Is so that all might live.
With you we will stay eternally
So Jesus, please, make us free.

TRIBUTE

A man's life,
For those looking on—
A definition of all he holds dear,
Spelled out with clarity—
Deeper than thought,
Plainer than utterance—
With actions, more than words.
Continually defining for us
The character of a leader,
With deeds of love,
Of dedication,
Of devotion,
Of duty and sacrifice!
On the well-worn knees of prayer
A body is built—
Strength of iron wrought
With the hardiest of ores!
A corruptible one bound
In the Armor of Light,
Standing incorruptible
As an exalted candle—
A seed of Light—
In a room despoiled with darkness!

I give tribute to a man,
Akin to this Light,
A life glorified by humble service
To an oft ungrateful people.
Tribute to a heart;
A heart jeweled—
Sparkling with the fruits
Of our Almighty Father's table!

continued

A Single Tomorrow in a Land of Yesterdays

One day I will stand as witness,
In the Golden Lands of heaven,
One of a multitude,
Giving tribute to a man's life—
My own eternity is largely due him,
And my own life I live—
As tribute!

MY REWARD

Though soon my body dies,
I look forward to my prize,
And though I am very old,
You promised streets of gold.

I will soon see my King,
And all eternity will I sing
Praises to the great and mighty Lord,
Finally, putting down my sword.

Many battles have we fought,
And through those fights were taught,
To trust in God and King,
And through all, He brings us singing!

To Him we go when we die,
And on Him I've set my eyes.
Not forgetting the promise spoken,
Never, Lord, to be broken!

I will walk with Him, on streets of gold,
Never again to be hot or cold.
In His kingdom I soon will dwell,
Escaping, forever, eternity in hell!

This promise you too can hold,
Before you become very old,
Because Jesus forgives all our sin,
Let new life and freedom begin!

So soon I will see the King,
And in His presence forever sing!
Don't forget to join me there,
I will meet you on the golden stair!

THE TRUMPET AND ITS THUNDER

Upon His throne all power resides,
He summons the saints to His side,
Searching for a Holy Nation,
He searches all of Creation.

Who will He find in this great blue world,
When in the sky His glory's unfurled?
All who lived lives for His pleasure
Will be gathered as golden treasure.

The sky will split, torn asunder,
With the Trumpet and its thunder,
A beckoning to His children,
And a finale to their selfish sin.

Who will He find in this Land of Lands,
To whom will He open His graceful hands?
All who in repentance called His name
Will be gathered up without blame.

Upon streets of gold His nation will dance,
Those who wasted not their only chance,
A day of joy, for those that made it,
An age of woe, for those His Word debated.

Will He find you on His Triumphant Return,
Or have you chosen the path of spurn?
Choose now to lay down your things,
And the King won't forget your offerings,
To His Kingdom we'll all be borne,
And in His arms our crowns adorned!

ONE DAY

One day the King, so noble and fair,
Descended from His lofty throne,
Naked and bare,
To save those who wander alone.

One day this King, so beautiful and bright,
Cast aside His crown,
And His splendid light,
As He humbly came down.

One day this King, perfect in everyway,
Took upon Himself
Those things we dare not say—
Those things we hide on our cluttered shelf.

One day my King, so very incorruptible,
Hanged in my place,
With mercy unbelievable,
Bearing my shame; my disgrace.

One day my King, unbroken and unashamed,
Took His throne once again,
King of the Blamed,
Freeing followers from the curse of sin!

And one day my King, so tried and so very true,
Will look upon you and I, His sons,
All those born anew,
Saying, "Well done, thy good and faithful ones!"

A Single Tomorrow in a Land of Yesterdays

ALL WHO SEE

"Arise my friend," I call to him,
With no reply I enter in,
Alone upon the floor he lies,
Blind to all who see with eyes,
Troubled no more by life's affairs,
Burdened not by past scares,
Blood spilled around him lies,
Blind to all who see with eyes,
No longer to hear my voice,
Death cares not what was his choice,
Lifeless upon the floor he lies,
Blind to all who see with eyes,
I know this death is not the end
Of my bitterly departed friend,
His spirit has left these skies,
Blind to all who see with eyes,
His road is traveled—choices made,
To the Lord his spirit bade,
Beyond this body his soul flies,
Blind to all who see with eyes,
This day his judgment passed—
This day which was his last,
Alone before the Throne he lies,
Blind to all who see with eyes,
He expected not his death,
Nor foresaw his last breath,
Alone with this last surprise,
Blind to all who see with eyes,
Alone to his last abode,
With his chosen load,
No more human guise,

Blind to all who see with eyes,
With this judgment past,
To heaven or hell is cast,
Alone to face his prize,
Blind to all who see with eyes!

A Single Tomorrow in a Land of Yesterdays

THE PROMISE BEYOND

Though a day of dread has come to us,
A time that none can foresee,
And a bitter parting has suddenly come,
We look to Heaven for the promise.

Questions pound our frail emotions:
What now? Where, from here, do we go?
And though it is not for us to know why,
Maybe we shall soon be shown.

But still our fear and doubts run,
Surging from deep within,
Though brief it may be,
We part painfully at last!

Our investment of love produces years of joy,
But fears are revealed in days of pain,
Though you leave us now
Your work was not in vain, nor unseen!

Your tears and sweat stain our floors,
And we weep at news of your parting.
All will bear fruit in its season,
And though we know not when, we desire it soon!

All words seem inadequate,
Mixing with tears of pain,
Yet here remains a joy beyond our grief,
And a promise—a promise of completion!

Though part we must,
May love remain and respect grow,
Though our paths be sundered
Friendship binds hearts across all borders!

A Single Tomorrow in a Land of Yesterdays

We know the best is yet to come
For the Lord, God, King of Heaven and Earth
Walks before us on our separate paths;
Be assured, where His hand guides blessings abound!

And so we look to the promise:
All prayers, hopes and dreams
Are in the hands of the Power of Heaven,
And with that, we rejoice in knowing you!

LOVE

YOUR WORDS

All your words read
As a love song to me!
You loved me more than self,
More than heaven's wealth!

Your life, a picture of words and deeds,
Point to you—the One the whole world needs,
You came from your Kingdom high above
Showing to all your endearing love,
A love that conquers all,
A love that will never fall,
You spoke to us as our father,
You spoke to us to bring us farther!

All your words read
As a love song to me!
You loved me more than self,
More than heaven's wealth!

You loved me more than all the earth,
You loved me before my birth,
You broke all bounds and chains,
You bought redemption with your pains,
As you breathed your last on that tree,
You broke all walls and set us free,
Your life and death and words given,
Are blessings, Lord, to all the living!

All your words read
As a love song to me!
You loved me more than self,
More than heaven's wealth!

I HAVE LOVED YOU

Before the foundations
Of the earth were laid,
Before the stars
Were set in their places,
And before the mountains
Were topped with snow,
I have loved you.
You were created for my love,
And by my love you were made.
For my love formed you,
And my love gave you life.
In no place,
In all of creation
Can you escape my love.
In life my love is shown,
And in death it is completed!
Before the planets
Were set in motion,
Before the moon
Accompanied the earth,
And before the great trees
Were called up from the soil,
I have loved you.
My love never dwindles,
Never fades.
My love never fails,
Never falters.
My love holds all together,
And by it all exists.
I have loved you,
Since before time,
Through all time,
And eternity,

A Single Tomorrow in a Land of Yesterdays

My love will remain true!
I have loved you,
With an everlasting love;
A love that conquers all things,
Endures all hardships,
And never, ever fails!
I have loved you!

INFINITE LOVE

Time continues on,
Without slipping or slowing,
Like a steam engine
It barrels on,
Never stopping.
Eventually all things end,
Time too will soon cease,
No more clocks,
Or jobs,
Or hours counted.
All restraint will be cast aside,
I will love you then
With an infinite love,
All eternity
Will seem inadequate—
Separation will pass,
I will always stand with you,
You will have to look no more.
For I will be wrapped,
Arms of love,
All around you,
Your eyes will finally open,
You will see my infinite love,
To no end.
Ages and ages will pass,
And still it will be
Just the dawn,
No dusk will come,
This is a love of a different world,
This is no romance,
Or fairy-tale story,
It is a story older than time itself,
A story beyond the beginning,
Beyond space and time—
All aspects of humanity.

A Single Tomorrow in a Land of Yesterdays

A story all have told,
Yet none experience, here.
I speak of love,
Infinite love.

A Single Tomorrow in a Land of Yesterdays

PURE LOVE

My love for you,
More pure than the purest gold,
And far more valuable,
Brighter than the brightest star,
And far nearer,
I surround you in my love,
Keeping fear and dread away.
My love for you,
Is the thread that holds,
The tie that binds,
The theme of all love songs.
All stories pale in comparison,
Mankind has little knowledge
Of the love
In which I speak.
Death cannot restrain it,
Pain cannot hold it back,
Time is just the beginning,
Eternity is needed for completion!
My love for you,
More powerful than the ocean,
And far more gentle,
Stronger than the shaking earth,
And far more endearing.
You can never escape my love,
I love you,
Through all rejection,
All rebellion,
All neglect,
And all denial.
For you, I traveled the heavens,
The earth, and the entire universe beyond!

A Single Tomorrow in a Land of Yesterdays

My love for you is pure,
Never faltering,
Never failing.
I have always,
And will always,
Love you!

SILENCE SPEAKS

When, in the silence—
Silent pondering in the still of night—
I wander this way, and that,
Through many memories
Long submerged—
Covered by cold, cruel waves of Forgetfulness,
And the merciless weight of Time—
I am reminded by the silence,
Of the story of our love;
Two souls collided with speed and fury,
In a perfect, unwavering love—
Love given by the Divine Influencer
Of men's hearts—
Joining two lives in the inseparable
Bond of matrimony.

Continuing this road of reminiscence,
Encouraged by the strength of Love—
Its overwhelming capacity
To overcome all obstacles unabated,
Heedless to the peril of intimacy—
Struck down only to return strengthened,
Avenged of the injury by Faithfulness,
And restored by the Almighty's slightest touch!
This Love, charged to our watch,
Shall not rest while Life's Breath remains,
Nor shall it fade in eternity,
For in His essence this Love exists,
And His Glory,
Like our love,
Shall never dwindle!

COMPANION

Brought together by omnipotent hands,
Blessed by His enduring grace,
Prospered by unbounded mercies,
Our lives connected by divine intent.

You are my every thought's companion,
Your blessing—my every deed's intention,
Our hearts united as one
In purpose, dream, and direction;
You are my constant, my devoted, companion!

Uncounted is the measure of our love,
True regardless of circumstance.
Borders are too small, and barriers too weak,
To long separate our unceasing love!

You are my every thought's companion,
Your blessing—my every deed's intention,
Our hearts united as one
In purpose, dream, and direction;
You are my constant, my devoted, companion!

Let no obstacle stand,
And no dream remain unachieved.
Let love bloom withered not,
For in this love is the beauty of constant growth.
There is none capable
Of parting our hearts, joined by God Himself!
Let none try to bar the way
For great is the wrath of Love's Defender,
And stern is the heart of stubborn love!

continued

A Single Tomorrow in a Land of Yesterdays

You are my every thought's companion,
Your blessing—my every deed's intention,
Our hearts united as one
In purpose, dream, and direction;
You are my constant, my devoted, companion!

DO YOU KNOW

Your smile sets the beat of my heart,
Your laughter gives my spirit wings,
From your eyes my gaze cannot depart,
Do you know the joy my love brings?

Your love is my life's companion,
Your presence is the height of my days,
Your voice is my inspiration,
Do you know that I love you, in all ways?

Your happiness is my treasure,
Your joy sets my life ablaze,
Your protection and peace is my pleasure,
Do you know I shall love you for all my days?

May the solidarity of my purpose and heart,
Give you faith in a love that remains true,
May time bring trust even when we are apart,
Do you know that forevermore I shall love you?

May the days of our love end only in death,
Let the time of our joy continually grow
So long as we have breath,
Do you know my love continues until my spirit I let go?

OF MY DREAM

In the Resting Lands of dream and fancy,
Beyond the wakeful watch of Reality,
Where in every minute there lies an age
Of fantastical plots, countless friends and foes,
There abides the Lady of my Dream.
A companion through all trials,
A beauty unsurpassed
In all corners of the far-stretching lands,
A lady of impeccable strength and character—
She stands fixed beyond my reach!
Thousands have I slain to become a Rescuer,
Strong towers I have built to be a Protector,
And countless beasts I have slain to be a Provider.
And yet this Lady of my Dream
Who dwells just within periphery,
Never, it seems, will she approach,
Nor allow me to draw nearer!
Always do I seek to be a hero,
That I might retain her attentive devotion,
And always do I fall helplessly short.
I thought my dream to be a dream of fancy,
Though it now seems an ever-threatening nightmare,
How shall I attain my Lady?
I have already drawn swords with her enemies,
And have always been the victor,
Countless foes have marched against my fortress;
Have I not vanquished them all?
Even hewing life and limb from the Serpent of Fire
Was not enough to gain my Prize!
This Lady alone had the power to elude capture,
And with all means I pursued ever stronger,
And in new ways:
A thousand verses I wrote and recited,
A field of roses I picked and delivered,
And renounced all acclaim as warrior, and king!

A Single Tomorrow in a Land of Yesterdays

Yet for all attempts I remained alone and destitute,
Until, beyond the borders of the Resting Lands,
In the bounds of Reality, she came to me!
This Lady of my Dream emerged from the mists and shadows,
Of doubt and disbelief,
And stood incarnate before me, in her familiar wondrous beauty!
And now you might ask,
'What became of this Lady of your Dream?'
My answer is quite simply this:
I have made her my bride!

THE JEWEL

You are the fulfillment of my desire;
You are the fan to the flaming fire.
You are the earthly prize I have always sought;
You are the jewel that can't be bought.

Your love was worth the wait;
The depth of this love: immeasurably great.
Your love deepens the meaning of life;
It soothes my pain and lessens my strife!

You are in my every thought and plan:
Your smile, and the touch of your hand.
Your face shines like the sun,
The night ends and a new day begun!

Your eyes shimmer as the stars above;
In the glimmer, I am graced by your great love.
Your every word is treasure to me,
You are my companion through life, into eternity.

You are the fulfillment of my desire;
You are the fan to the flaming fire.
You are the earthly prize I have always sought;
You are the jewel that can't be bought.

You are worth more than gold and silver,
You are my love, and I am your lover.
You are whom I hold dearest,
As life stretches forth, I hold you nearest!

Your eyes are holding my future;
In them is my life's pleasure.
As you give a mirror reflection,
You gaze upon my object of affection!

A Single Tomorrow in a Land of Yesterdays

You are the jewel of the King's crown,
I have picked you up never to lay you down.
In my arms you will always stay!
None can steal my jewel away!

You are the fulfillment of my desire;
You are the fan to the flaming fire.
You are the earthly prize I have always sought;
You are the jewel that can't be bought.

ALLOW ME

Allow me the pleasure,
If only for a short while,
For this life passes all too quickly,
To wrap my loving arms around you,
To weave for you a blanket
With the threads of my love,
To keep out life's bitter cold,
And the frost shall not bite you,
No winter's wind may penetrate,
For I weave it with the very warmth—
The essence of my heart.

Allow me the pleasure,
If only for this lifetime,
For time slows not,
And death hurries ever nearer,
To walk with you in life,
To be your companion,
Your guard that stands by with ready sword,
For none shall avail in ending my love,
None may creep in to steal you,
Evading my wrath,
My love for you beats with its own heart,
And is cold as iron for our enemies,
We shall be as one,
United with unbreakable love!

Allow me to build for you,
With all my heart and strength,
A stronghold in the realm of my love,
A fortress of power and peace,
Every stone carved with the thought of you,
Walls that stand high above this barren land,

A Single Tomorrow in a Land of Yesterdays

All things in this realm
Are, indeed, blessed and graced by you,
I alone stand watch with love,
And grow not weary in my cause—to love you,
And forsake all others!

THE GIFT

Lord of Heaven and Earth,
I just want to thank you for the gift.
She is my sun,
In my sunless day,
She is my strength,
When my own fails,
She is my friend,
When I am abandoned.
She is my light,
When my own dims,
She is my voice,
When my own vanishes.
Lord, I thank you for the gift!
When I am broken,
She mends,
When I feel alone,
She stands beside,
When I fail,
She forgives.
When I am down,
She pulls me up,
When I feel pain,
She is my soothing.
Lord God, and Gracious Father,
Thank you for the gift,
Thank you
For my companion,
And friend!
She is more to me
Than I ever expected.
I love her now
As I love myself!
We share thoughts,
We share dreams
And desires.

A Single Tomorrow in a Land of Yesterdays

She is beautiful in all ways!
And in all ways I love her,
Completely,
And with no end!
In all ways I thank you, Lord,
For the gift

I DO

As one awestruck by the dawn—
Eyes fixed, immobile—
Helplessly I gaze upon
The only one who could fulfill
The dreams I've dared dream,
Of the bride, beauty-laden—
Dress of white, veiled smile sheen—
Doubt not my Beauty's beauty pervading!
Having done, and said, all that might woo
All that remains is the formal: "I do".

LIFE IN LOVE

Promises have been made,
Some kept; some broken,
The word of man is weak and volatile,
It is given sincerely,
And too often sincerely forgotten,
Like a cloud of smoke driven by the wind,
Dissipated into a million invisible things,
Given without thought of consequence for neglect,
Breaking hearts and trust, and faith in fellow man!

But to you my word I give
With all thought and devotion,
My mouth wary of the words,
Mindfully forced to count neglect as death,
My word I give as no other thing,
For I am bound to it,
And it carries me through all trials,
I will never forget nor neglect,
Lest death carries me blindly away!

This is my pledge to you:
I will give you my whole heart,
Or I will die in the process,
My love will reach you beyond all things,
It will be a lasting remnant of my word and soul,
If my love fades, so also will my life.
I will give you a love in life,
And a life in love!

continued

A Single Tomorrow in a Land of Yesterdays

Though life is complicated,
And I am battered with struggles,
There is one thing that remains constant,
Forever simplifying,
I love you beyond measure,
And nothing in my life, or in yours,
Can take away my promise—
To love you through all life!

My pledge remains and is true:
My love will reach you beyond all things,
It will be a lasting remnant of my word and soul,
If my love fades, so also will my life
I give you a love in life,
And a life in love!

CHILDREN

TREASURE OF MINE

To you, my Lord, I return
This precious treasure,
Wondering why to me it was entrusted!

What have I done to earn
Something of this worth?
A gift above the reaches
Of this tiny Earth,
Stretching ever on,
Into a future beyond my own,
With my life I guard it—
Never to leave it alone!

To you, my Lord, I return
This precious treasure,
Wondering why to me it was entrusted!

How does a gift this small
Carry so much weight?
And with such responsibility,
Make the good great,
You have with this treasure
Reached the pinnacle of design,
Breathing the Breath of life
Into this child, and treasure, of mine!

BLESSED EMERGENCE

When before our great Lord I stand,
Among the most blest
I shall count myself
Most bestowed in all that Holy Land!

From among them my humble pride shown
Not above the rest—
Boasting not of self—
But of this, my little one, whom I have known.

For my heart has beheld a future queen,
Hands have touched,
Right arm guarded—
In her eyes, the King's maiden I have seen.

I speak of joy beyond this world's words,
Future touched,
And evil thwarted—
Heart ever resounds with her dear voice heard!

To you, my daughter, I surrender my heart,
Forget not my effort
When you have grown;
Let no thing, conquering love, drive us apart.

Always, I will thank the Lord for our convergence,
Forever to support
The seeds He has sown—
Blessed gift of life, blessed daughter, blessed emergence!

SMILES RETURNED

A simple reminder of grace given me—
Smile returned by this little one I see—
How we, your children, must appear from above,
When viewed through an atmosphere of love!
With this child given me, I begin to understand
Just what is meant by, 'walking hand in hand'—
His little fingers firmly grasping, holding mine;
A reflection of mine in yours, both stories sanguine!
For in you, I find what he finds in me,
The depths of: strength, hope, peace, love, and security.
In his eyes I see boundless future unfolding,
Praying your blessings upon him—none withholding!

My Lord, watch this one when I cannot,
And keep him from the Destroyer's plot,
May the strength of your right hand upon him rest,
And the labors of his life be forever blest!
I ask not for the presence of angels by his side,
But that your Spirit dwell in his heart, ever to abide.
Make me, Dear Lord, the father he requires everyday,
That I might fail not the instruction of your way.
With open eyes, I lift this prayer to you, with a smile—
May he remember, through laughs and cries, all the while
The smile that graces his face has never been ignored,
But at all times, been returned him by you, my Lord!

A Single Tomorrow in a Land of Yesterdays

NO CLAIM

And though we sought in earnest
No less a miracle
Than creation itself—
A treasure, nonetheless,
Of more value than all worlds,
All hoards of treasure—
Unto you we commend it!
How could we deny you your own, my Lord?
Giving you all years awaiting—
All futures, firsts, beginnings, and ends;
All things wrapped snugly—
Almost secretly—
Within this tiniest of bundles.
As we hold aloft in your court,
What tears of sadness,
Tears of joy,
And prayers uncounted
Have birthed with miracles,
And merriment—
Beyond the sway of shadow and cloud—
In the Land of Eternal Dawn
This form which cries praise above
The faint recollection of pains unspeakable,
Though diminished,
In the light of new life and limbs!
Be this child ever your child;
We have no claim
But what you graciously give!
And though we sought in earnest
No less a miracle
Than creation itself—
A treasure, nonetheless,
Of more value than all worlds,
All hoards of treasure—
Unto you we commend it!

STORIES

I MET A MAN

∽

I am a traveler; I have wandered many a mile in search of something. Although, I was quite unsure of what, or whom, I was so intensely seeking. My purpose was to find happiness, not a just a fun time, but true joy. This happiness was somehow evading me, no matter how deeply I sought to find it. I pursued this ideal—this utopia—high and low, in daylight and dark. My future was certain despite my rough road. I would find perfect peace, though I knew not where to look. All I needed was a guide.

One day during my travels on this rugged road, I met what seemed to me the most beautiful person. This man was tall and stately—so inviting to look upon. He was dressed in a garment like I had never seen before; it seemed to change hue as the breeze moved upon it. Its color at times shined like the sun, and yet at times, as he walked toward me, seemed to absorb all light. This was a very, very intriguing man. His very presence demanded my respect, for in him there was a hidden power—a power far beyond the strength of his form. It was indeed a pleasure to meet such a man.

So I asked him to join me on my rocky path, but he declined and said, "I cannot go that way, but you may join me, for you seem weary in your search. I will help you find what you seek. My way is much, much easier."

I longed to join him, yet I desired to find my own path. I was my own master, and I relied on no one but myself. I knew in my heart that leaving my road would result in failure. So for now we parted ways. I took my hard and perilous road and he his own path. I watched from a distance as he walked slowly away. My eyes were drawn to him, and I stood unable to withdraw my gaze until long after he passed from my sight. My heart raced as I thought of running to join him, but I shook it off. I turned my back to him, continuing on alone.

It was not long until I met that man again. Our roads traveled side by side for some miles, so we were able to walk together. What I enjoyed most about him was his wonderful voice. We walked and talked together until my road veered off, and once again he graciously asked me to journey with him. So sincere he seemed when he claimed he would miss my company—his voice silky smooth and his words so enticing—that I could not refuse. So I joined this wonderful man.

As we walked together, conversing all the while, I noticed him hiding his eyes. This matter was a puzzle that I wished for quick resolution. Why would a man of his apparent power and beauty hide his eyes? A man's eyes are a porthole to his soul and purpose.

I soon took little notice of this, for his voice was intoxicating and his path was so easy that I almost fell fast asleep as I walked beside him. After enjoying his company for some time I desired to find my original road. I knew my mission, and this was not helping it. Somehow, here I was lacking something. It was great to be with him, yet I had not found that peace I longed for. I begged leave of my newly found friend and bid him farewell.

This he did not foresee and for a second unveiled his eyes. They shone red, like a fire was burning deep within! And for a moment all light seemed captured by his anger, as he appeared viciously dark and savage. At first his voice was hideously twisted, then softened to his normal fluid-like voice. It was as if he had stopped the rushing flow of a mighty river!

"No, please stay with me. It is so easy here. You are tired. You cannot leave.

You must camp here with me tonight. I will guide you to what you desire, to joy and peace. You have business to attend, I know, but tonight you rest in peace. I will not leave your side, my friend. You are safe!"

Once again, I could decline. After all, he was so convincing, and for some reason I feared to leave his side. Without him it seemed I had nothing, but with him I thought I finally had a piece of what I sought. In our short time together I grew to love his presence. He spoke of things contrary to what I had learned, though he seemed so right and true, at least, here on this simple, easy road. All seemed right with this man, and I could offer no argument for I believed every word. My friend had obviously been well educated. Words fell from his lips like honey; I greatly anticipated hearing every one.

I had to daily awaken myself mentally to realize truth. I was definitely enjoying the newly found wisdom given me freely by my companion, and friend. My desire for him grew daily stronger. I had, may I say, a lust for his presence, his voice, and his company! My time became dream-like with him. Still, I informed him that when morning came I would be returning to my former path.

That night I dreamed horrible, terrifying dreams! It seemed that as I slept I saw my friend looking down upon me. His eyes, unveiled the second time, watched me, reflecting the firelight, but this fire in his eyes was too strong a blaze; it seemed it would catch the entire forest in its flame!

But wait! We had set no fire!

I jumped from my sleep, heart pounding and drenched in sweat, only to find my friend standing over a campfire cooking a delightful breakfast. I was greatly relieved, but still excited. Covering my face, to hide my horror, I ran to the stream to wash up. My reflection did not show the happiness I had been feeling, only the shock and fear of my uneasy sleep. Where was my peace—my joy? When I returned I found I was not the only one affected by the night.

"Awake, awake my friend. Did you not sleep well," he laughed. But his voice seemed harsh and rude, and his knowing laughter sent chills down my spine!

I ate his breakfast in silence only awaiting a chance to leave, and a good enough reason to do so; my recent fear of him would not suffice. I was confused by his transformation, and now his very presence seemed to darken all light around. I grew more fearful moment by moment. A mist surrounded us, settling heavily upon my heart.

"There is a fog this morning," he said, "Maybe I should lead you back to your lonely, stony path. I fear you will be unable to find it in the mist. For I know this country very well, and it is very perilous off the road, in the mists!"

I remained silent, struggling for a way out of this, finding none. He made all things irresistible. His voice still had not returned to its former beauty. He blamed this on the warm, dank air of the forest. Everything seemed to grow darker and drearier—bleak and ominous—as we continued on together: I in fear, and my 'friend' enjoying every darkening step.

For as we continued onward the darkness grew and grew as if we traveled to the very heart of darkness! Not only did the darkness increase, but so also did my anxiety and longing to leave. My strength to resist him dwindled to practically nothing when, finally, I confronted my new leader. I asked him why we had not yet reached my road.

"You do not have a road, my slave. You will travel where I lead," was his horrifying answer.

He said this unmasking his true voice and self! A voice like the very voice of treachery and hatred now harassed me. At that moment I felt the crush of steel on my ankles and wrists.

"You are mine now, slave. No one can free you now. Just try to escape!" His voice froze my body in fear and his laughter cut to my heart.

Now he was truly unveiled in all his evil. His eyes were red as blood and shone like fire. His body only intensified the utter darkness around us. His claws were as a lions tipped with malice, and in his mouth he revealed a forked tongue and daggers for teeth! Just to look upon him now was perilous. His presence inspired pain, torment, fear, and evil.

He leapt upon me, slashing me to the bone. My pain was his pleasure and my torment his delight. The forest all around seemed to turn and flee from him. This beast I once called friend—now captor—continued to drive me slowly on. As my pain broke me, he only inflicted more, laughing all the while.

I had never known about such evil before, yet I realized then this was my own fault. I could have turned away at any time. I could have said no. Instead, I allowed this thing to fill my mind with his lies and confusion.

A Single Tomorrow in a Land of Yesterdays

In the midst of my torture I heard the rattle of chains. Unbeknownst to me, the chains were mine! Shackles had been clamped on my ankles and wrists! I had no hope of freedom or life; I was his! All around me was the stench of death and decay. The darkness, and the sense of hopelessness increased without bounds.

My captor sliced me within inches of my life, until he was forced to carry me! I sought, I yearned, and I longed for a way to freedom, but it was not in my strength. Total despair filled my being. It drove me mad that I had been such a fool! I writhed in pain to free myself.

"You need not struggle, my captive, for I own you now! I will torture you until your Creator knows you not! I am your destruction! I am your demise!" He said this with wicked pleasure, with eminent force and power.

In my torment I looked around; to find I was being carried to prison. All around were helpless people like me, great and small, with captors much like mine. Some were hideously transfigured by their malice and wickedness. Some longed for a way of escape as I did. And some were leaving!

What is this? There is a way out!

Then I saw Him, a man of power and beauty like no other. A man of light, not of darkness, of love not hatred or malice! This man did not cover His eyes or His intent,

He longed to free the captive not torture them. Thousands were standing around Him thanking Him for their freedom; he dressed them all in brilliant white garments. I would have given everything to be one of those standing next to him, covered by His brilliant light.

A ray of His light fell upon me, exposing the grotesque ugliness of my situation. Bound by an expert jailor, I had no hope for freedom! I was bleeding, bruised, with no strength left, and what is more, I was to blame. I longed to speak, when a powerful voice called out from behind us.

"Call to Him!" was all it said. I truly believed He was the only way out, but I could only manage a whisper for Him to save me! As I was carried, my captor flung me down, and shrunk back, thrashing about in fear.

The man of Light was approaching!

"You cannot have him," the beast cried out, looking up at the man of Light, in great terror. "He is mine. I own him. I will destroy him. I have…"

"Silence!" Said this man of righteousness, " You have nothing! You have no authority over him! I paid for him. Do you not remember? I have the keys to these cells. I have the power to forgive him. Flee from my presence! I will deal with you another day!"

My captor fled in fear and pain, and my chains were broken, by grace, in the power of this Holy man's light.

"Come, my son, let me show you the path away from destruction. I have set you free, and now you must follow me. I will never leave your side or forsake you to this place of doom and judgment. For I am the judge of all, and you have been pardoned by my grace through your faith. Keep your eyes on the road ahead, and I will keep you strong."

So, now I follow the King, my Savior, and the Lord of Light! The freed people march with him, in light, destroying this world of darkness, and freeing the captives, as I was freed.

THE BOY AT THE ALTAR

~

One night, as I was preparing for bed, God showed me something; He shined on me His heavenly light, and revealed this precious story to me. This story is the story of all those who come to God—all those who come to Him seeking forgiveness and redemption. The Lord's own Holy Spirit showed to me this story of salvation.

I seemed to be looking, in heaven, at God seated on His throne of power and judgment. There before me, seated on high, was the Most High God, King of all creation! The brilliance and essence of God is completely indescribable, and words in any language are irrelevant. Just to think of the King of Kings, in all of His exceeding glory, was, and still is, mind-boggling.

All around His throne were angels singing His Praise, bowing in His Presence. At His right hand, the hand of power and authority was His son Jesus. Even though I was looking on from a distance, the sight of this place and God Himself, the view struck my heart with fear and awe. The beauty all around was like nothing ever seen; everything shone from the glory of God, and all heaven seemed lit by His presence!

After a few moments of taking in this powerful sight, my eyes seemed to adjust to the brightness. Beside me stood an angel, or maybe the Holy Spirit; I do not know which. This tall and beautiful being slowly stretched out his arm, as if pointing to the foot of God's throne. At that moment, I noticed that the angels surrounding the throne were also looking to where he pointed, though they did not cease praising Him. God Himself was looking down toward His own feet. Compelled to know what they were now intently gazing at, my heart seemed as if it would thunder out of my chest!

Jesus was the only one looking up, and He was looking directly at me. He motioned to me to come closer; I could not have refused if I had wished, for my spirit almost left my body as I ran to the Father's feet. When I reached God's feet I could not help but look up at Him. His throne and His body, up to His mighty shoulders, were clearly and impressively visible, but the view of His face was completely blocked by His impermeable glory. Jesus looked much the same, but I could see His smiling face as He gazed deep into my soul. I thought that His gaze would literally break me, and then He, along with the angels, turned toward His Father's feet.

I turned my gaze from Jesus to look at the foot of the Almighty, and right then I understood what they were all looking at. There before God's feet was an opening torn through the very fabric of heaven; it was a window to the earth below. I came closer, and leaning in, I peered through this window, not knowing what I would see!

At first, I saw earth from a distance in outer space. The view through this 'window' changed as it quickly sped toward earth. I saw the moon pass and the clouds of earth's atmosphere. The view raced closer and closer to the surface; I saw a town, and what appeared to be a church in this town. The now somewhat clouded view penetrated the roof of this building and eventually stopped right below the ceiling.

Now I saw a congregation, seated in chairs and facing a stage, where a speaker eloquently spoke from God's word. As the view cleared I immediately recognized my own church, though it has changed much since that time. Only faintly did I recognize people, partly because of the strange viewing angle and partly because what I now saw happened many years ago. I looked up, noticing God Himself on the edge of His seat; He was very intent on what I was watching—what all of heaven seemed to be watching. I was about to ask why I was being shown this part of my past, but my answer was spoken before I could form the words.

"All will be shown, in due time. Now watch and listen." Came my answer in the form of an exceedingly powerful voice, which shook me to the very bone.

A Single Tomorrow in a Land of Yesterdays

Up until that point the only sound I had heard were the angels praising God, but now I could hear every sound as I watched this view unfold before me. The speaker spoke of God's love, Jesus' sacrifice, forgiveness of sins, and also prophecies of the Second Coming.

While this man spoke I noticed something in the congregation. Somewhere close to the middle there was an intense light, but it did not come from the church's interior lights. Instead, it came from a seat where a small boy sat; the light seemed to be wrapped around this child over and over, blanketing him from any source of external, or internal, darkness. Although this light hid the boy's features I could plainly see that he was focused upon God's spoken word, and he was oblivious to any distractions. God inaudibly revealed to me that this light surrounding the boy was God's protection and conviction; the Holy Spirit was with him, and was preparing him for something.

While the service continued, the light grew in intensity, to the point where it was almost blinding to look at! I assumed the preacher was an evangelist because I did not recognize him as my own pastor. His sermon drew to a conclusion, and he began to give an altar call. At this point the bright light filled the entire sanctuary with its brilliance, sweeping away all remnants of shadow. It then moved toward the altar, and still it grew brighter. I could not look directly into the light, yet I could not look away for I was compelled to look. From the depths of my soul I could not force myself to look away! Just then the light exploded, shards of it sped through space and up through my viewing window! I was thrown flat on my back at the Savior's feet!

All at once, all heaven broke loose in celebration! I looked at Jesus who was grinning from ear to ear, and speaking excitedly to the Father in some sweet heavenly language. This language flowed, like the very ocean up and down, in cadence of power and authority. All heaven was enamored by what had happened, and God the Father and Jesus His son, were at the epicenter of an earthquake of celebration! In a place where joy and peace envelope all things this was a pinnacle of epic proportions!

I longed deeply to know what I had missed, so I crawled to the window to peer in. I was amazed at what I saw! Now the boy I had seen earlier filled the view; he was at the altar, and he was weeping without restraint. I was now facing him as he sobbed, face buried in the altar. Up until that moment, I was still confused as to the purpose of this sight, and then, in an instant, it was all made crystal clear to me! For the boy lifted his head from the altar, tears streaming down both sides of his face, and I saw in him my own face, many years younger!

I gasped for air, and it seemed I would find none. I realized then that it was I God had prepared for salvation. That night, in that church, God had sent His Holy Spirit to touch my life eternally! His light had surrounded me and protected me from all darkness, internal and external. Not only did God call me to Himself by His Spirit, but also when I did reach God, through Jesus His son, all heaven broke out in joyous celebration! All that celebration was for just one little boy, at an altar, who admitted his sins and asked Jesus to be Lord of his life!

ONLY A BOY

∽

Jesse was an old man, he was feeble, and he did not travel well anymore. So Jesse called his youngest son, David, from the field where he was tending the sheep. He told David to prepare some food and supplies for his brothers.

Jesse was greatly concerned about his three oldest sons: Eliab, Abinadab, and Shammah. They had been camped in the Valley of Elah for forty days, and Jesse wanted assurance from them; assurance that Israel would defeat its enemy, the Philistines, and assurance that his sons would not die. Jesse, being old in years, would rather die than see one of his sons die first.

"David, my boy," Jesse said to David as he just finished packing the supplies for his journey, "take these things to your brothers, and take these ten cheeses to their commander. Find out for me, David, how your brothers are holding out. Bring word as soon as you can!"

"I will do as you say, father." David replied in obedience as if standing before God himself, "I will bring word as soon as possible." Jesse looked down, his face bearing the concern he felt, so David continued. "Father, do not worry. They will be fine. How can our enemies defeat us when we have been chosen by Jehovah?"

"You are right my son! Now go and hurry back. For I long to have news."

David left his father's side hurrying for the Valley of Elah, where the Israelite army was encamped. David knew exactly where the encampment was located, for he had been in service to the king for months now. Saul, the king of Israel, had suffered lately of an evil spirit, and David played the harp for king Saul to soothe him when the evil spirit overcame him. It troubled David that Israel's king would be under this spirit. It also troubled David that someday Saul might find out about Samuel's visit to David.

Just a few short weeks before, God's servant, Samuel, visited Jesse's household. While David was in the field, Samuel came to offer a sacrifice to Jehovah. Samuel consecrated each of Jesse's sons, except for David, and asked them to join him in the sacrifice. When they came to the place for the sacrifice Samuel had each of Jesse's sons pass in front of him.

After they had passed by, Samuel asked Jesse, "Are there no more? Do you have no more sons?"

"There is but one. He is the youngest, and now he watches over the sheep." David's brothers chuckled at this.

"Send for him. I would very much like to see him." Commanded Samuel.

This caused David's brothers to wonder, "Why had they been passed over?"

When David arrived, he was very surprised to see the servant of Almighty standing before him, and Samuel said, "This is the one." To the shock of everyone, Samuel took a horn of oil, anointing David's head.

David received this anointing very humbly, though he knew what it meant; God had chosen him to succeed Saul as king of Israel. From that moment on, as before, the Lord and Creator of the entire universe walked with David. Jehovah's very presence walked with David, and it empowered him to do great deeds.

This is what worried David. For if Saul found that he would someday be replaced as king, by the same boy that played the harp for him, he might try to kill David. Watching the anointing had already affected the way David's own brother's treated him; what would that news do to a king already afflicted by an evil spirit? David placed his worries in the back of his mind as he approached the Valley of Elah.

"Nothing bad can happen to me," David thought, "for I have been anointed by God's own servant. Why would Jehovah anoint me to have me killed?"

A Single Tomorrow in a Land of Yesterdays

David reached the encampment as the battle lines were drawn and the battle cries were sounded. The Philistines and the Israelites walked to their battle positions facing each other. In order to work up the courage to battle in this brutal and vicious way, the opposing armies would shout challenges to each other. This made an enemy's blood boil and the battle would ensue.

David left the supplies with the keeper and ran to his brothers in the battle lines. David began to talk with his brothers. He asked them how they were and how the battle was going. He could see no signs of war; there were no dead on the battlefield, no wounded in the camp. As he was talking to his brothers, a giant philistine, over nine feet tall, walked to the front of the Philistine lines. This Philistine wore massive bronze armor that glimmered brightly in the mid-morning sunlight, and he carried a huge sword and spear; before him walked a shield bearer. This giant walked forward and issued a challenge to the Israelite army.

"Would you prepare for battle?" The giant began, shouting across the field, his voice full of arrogance, "I am Goliath, and before me you are all like sheep led to slaughter. I am a Philistine. Aren't you the servants of Saul, king of Israel?" Goliath burst out laughing and continued, "Choose a man, if you have any in your camp, and send him out to challenge me. If he can kill me," Goliath again laughed a defiant laugh, "we will become your servants. But if I win, and win I shall, you will become our servants. This day I defy all the ranks of Israel! You are nothing before me! Send a man to me, if there are any among you. Now, that I might kill him!"

With that last word the Israelites, all but David, were filled with terror. The Israelite battle lines collapsed on each other as the entire army retreated in fear. The captains of the army commanded their men to return to the lines, and they did, but not nearly as far forward as before.

David asked a man nearby, "Who is this Philistine to defy the army of the Holy One of Israel? What will be done for the man who removes this disgrace from the battlefield?"

Before the man could answer Eliab, David's oldest brother, overheard, and growing very angry stepped in, saying, "Why are you here, boy? Go back to tending your sheep. You know nothing of battle, so go home. You only came here to watch us die in battle, while you gloat!"

"I have done nothing!" David responded, "Now allow me to speak!" David turned his back to his brother, and again asked, "What will the king do for the one who slays this man, this wicked Philistine who defies the name of Almighty God?"

The man David spoke to now answered, "This vile Philistine comes out to challenge us everyday, for forty days. Each day the king tells us that any man who kills the giant will be given great riches! The king will also give his daughter in marriage, and he will exempt the man and his family from paying taxes"

A man walked up behind David, tapping him on the shoulder. David turned and expecting to see his brother, was shocked to see the king's messenger. The messenger looked at David, saying, "Saul, our king anointed by God's servant, would speak with you, David."

David was then instructed to follow the messenger to the king's tent. This time it felt strange, awkward, and uncomfortable, to be taken into the familiar presence of the king. How did Saul know that David was there? Why did Saul want to see him? Had Saul learned of the anointing? It wasn't David's day of service, and he did not have his harp with him.

He came into the king's tent, but before Saul could speak, David, empowered by the Lord, boldly said, "Let no one lose strength of heart! This Philistine is of no consequence. He defies the One True God, and surely he deserves death! It will be put off no longer; I, David your servant, will destroy this Philistine champion!"

The king's mouth fell open, as did those of all who heard. Saul then looked at David, standing before him as if he were a bold warrior, and said, "You cannot fight this Philistine! For you are only a boy, and this Philistine has been a warrior since he was your age. No, you cannot fight him. For you will be killed and all will be lost!"

"Only a boy! Only a boy, you say? How can you say that when the Lord God Almighty stands with me? Can you not see that this Philistine has been given unto me by the hand of the Lord most High?" David could not contain himself, "I, your servant, have continually watched my father's flock, and when danger comes deliverance is given to me by the Lord's hand. The bear and the

A Single Tomorrow in a Land of Yesterdays

lion both took lambs from the flock, and the bear and the lion are both carcasses because of it! I struck them and plucked from their mouths the stolen lambs. And though they turned on me, I stand before you now, my king. For I struck them until they died in my hands! The Lord delivered me from these creatures, and now the Lord will deliver me from this wicked Philistine! For this man blasphemes the Lord Almighty!"

So Saul resigned his stance and took heed to David's words. "Go, and God keep you from harm! Also take my armor to protect you." Saul said with a slight and sincere smile.

After putting on Saul's armor David walked around trying it out. David did not feel comfortable in the armor; it was much too large for him, and he could not wield Saul's sword.

As David took off the armor he told the king, "I cannot use this armor or your sword. Do not fear for me, or the army of the Lord, for our Holy God will deliver us this very day!"

With that, David took his staff and ran to a nearby stream where he quickly chose five smooth stones. Placing the stones in his pouch, he pulled out his sling, and took off running for the front of the battle lines. David stopped just in front of the foremost line. While David had run to the front line the Philistine realized that he finally had a challenger, and he slowly walked forward with his shield bearer in front. David's heart was filled with emotion—anger—because this Philistine had challenged the Lord himself.

As David walked forward he prayed out loud, "Jehovah, my God and Provider, keep me now, your servant, safe from evil; even as I desire to crush your enemies with your might. Deliver unto me this day, Goliath, your enemy! Thank you for my victory!"

David now approached the Philistine, armed with only a staff and sling; Goliath looked him over and laughed. "Am I a dog, that you might beat me with mere sticks and stones?" He laughed defiantly, "Come here, boy, that I might strike you down and feed your bones to the birds and wild animals!" Goliath began to curse David by the power of his gods, and all the Philistine army resounded with battle cries.

David was filled with anger and with power from Almighty, the Just. He looked Goliath straight in the eyes as he walked toward him, and said, "You come against me with the power of your sword and your spear, but I come against you with the power of Jehovah, the Almighty and everlasting God of heaven and earth! Today, Goliath, you will die by the hand of the Lord, for he has delivered you into my hand! Today, you will be food for the birds and wild animals, and I will carry your head as my trophy! For you have defied the armies of the God of Israel, and for that you must, and surely, will die!"

All of the Israelite army jumped forth, rallying their battle cry! Each man was filled with courage after hearing David's courageous and confident words; all of them now understood that the Almighty Jehovah was on their side. Then Goliath became enraged and advanced to engage David in battle. David, not waiting for the Philistine, dropped his staff and ran with courage out to meet him. He armed his sling as he ran, and swung it with all his might, aimed directly for the Philistine's head. The stone sank deeply into Goliath's forehead just between his eyes. The giant stumbled a little. All eyes focused on this battle in the middle of the valley saw the miracle! Goliath blinked twice, and then his eyes closed for the final time. The mighty giant fell face down crushing his own shield bearer!

All the Philistine army ran in fear and dismay; they had surely lost! David, forgetting not his words before the battle, quickly ran out to where Goliath lay, atop his shield bearer. He drew that huge sword from its scabbard, and lifted it high above his own head, looked up to see the Israelite army pursuing the fleeing Philistines. David brought down that mighty sword with all his might upon Goliath's neck, and the head came free of the giant's huge shoulders! It was as David had declared; he carried Goliath's head as his trophy!

The Lord gave the Israelites the victory that day! They demolished the Philistine army, and left their carcasses for the birds and wild animals. The dead Philistines were strewn everywhere along the Shaaraim road all the way to Gath and Ekron. The Israelite army looted the Philistine camp, and David took for himself the weapons of the Philistine giant. The Lord blessed David that day and continued to bless him to the end of his earthly days, as king of the chosen ones of Israel! And David became a man after God's own heart.

THE HEALER

~

Stythenes had always traveled with an extensive caravan. He was a man of vast resources; though, it had not always been this way. Something, or someone, had brought many blessings upon him. Stythenes had always been ambitious, trying to make more of what he was given, and on this trip to Jerusalem he sought to bring an abundant profit.

"Gain is the root of my happiness," Stythenes often told himself; though, he never seemed to find that happiness.

Stythenes, and his entire household, traveled the main trade route south toward Korazin of Galilee. There in Korazin they would take their rest, and continue on to Jerusalem, where they would trade their goods for money and supplies. Many menservants and maidservants traveled with Stythenes for he owned much and required much help.

He was a man of honor, and did not mistreat these servants, even though they were his property. Stythenes needed them, and they needed him; his servants cared for his many horses, cattle, donkeys, sheep and goats. In return, Stythenes provided them with food and shelter, and, not to mention, a meager wage of their own. They had seen much on their journey so far: mountains, rivers, lakes, and masses of people traveling the great trade route. However, nothing they had seen could prepare them for what they would see the following day.

Stythenes was pleased with the progress they made; they had already neared Korazin. So now, he sought to find a campsite to rest for the night. He called to his faithful servant Jophine.

A Single Tomorrow in a Land of Yesterdays

"Come here, my good Jophine," Stythenes commanded, "go on ahead and find a suitable ground for such a caravan as we are. Take Menes, my fastest horse, and hurry. For the sun will soon be down, and we will be covered by darkness!"

"Yes, good master," replied Jophine, "I will do just as you say."

Quickly, Jophine mounted Menes, and raced toward the foot of a mountain up ahead. The rest of the company followed Jophine at a slower rate, and before long Menes and Jophine pulled up beside Stythenes on the lead horse.

"There is a beautiful spot of ground just ahead," exclaimed Jophine, "it is at the foot of the mountain, and in perfect view of the Sea of Galilee. It is not far. We have enough time, before the sun sets, even at this pace, master."

This brought a smile to Stythenes' face. "Thank you, good Jophine. You are truly a blessing to me. When we reach this spot we will set up camp for the night, and kill a fatted calf for a celebration of my son's birthday!"

Jophine smiled, and nodded, returning to his fellow servants to prepare them as they reach the campsite. Jophine, and the men, began to work at once setting up the tents. They also cared for the livestock, and prepared to slaughter a calf for the feast. The women set to work on the meal, and all the campsite was busy with work. Stythenes, his wife and son, worked right along with the servants in all they did. Stythenes could never forget the life of the workingman, and he desired to make it easier for all.

This night was a joyous occasion, filled all with joy and laughter. Stythenes stood to bring the celebration to an end, amidst sighs of disappointment.

"All good things must come to an end," he sadly proclaimed, "and it is very late. But do not forget why we have come from our distant land. We have come to make a profit so that our lives might be filled with all that we desire. So, goodnight to all and may we wake refreshed and enthused by this joyous celebration! And to my boy, may this milestone carry you even closer to manhood. Goodnight all!"

So to bed they all proceeded, content in heart and anxious about the next day's travel. They all slept beautifully, for all were very pleased. With all the night's activities, and all the wearisome trav-

A Single Tomorrow in a Land of Yesterdays

eling, the entire company slept well past dawn. The first to awaken was Jophine; soon afterwards he stood over his master's bed, and whispered, "wake, master, wake up. It is late in the day and the sun is well on its way."

Stythenes awoke with a jump, grabbing Jophine by the throat! He quickly realized what he was doing and released Jophine. "I am so sorry, my faithful servant! Please forgive your master, but you have truly startled me."

"You are forgiven, master." Jophine said with a red face, "But master you must get up. The morning is quickly fading away, and we have all slept late. I have awakened all the servants and they are preparing us to leave, but we waste time here! I am sorry for my intrusion, master, but I did not know what else to do."

"You have done well, Jophine, thank you. Now my family and I must prepare for our journey." Stythenes said with gladness as he walked Jophine to the tent entrance.

Stythenes wasted no more time. He woke his family, and they prepared to leave in a matter of moments. So the caravan was soon ready to depart the foot of that mountain in the bright mid-morning sunlight. All around the campsite were people walking up the face of the mountain, forming a crowd at the feet of a man seated upon a rock. Stythenes saw this as an opportunity to make a profit, so he halted his caravan for a closer look.

He quickly placed a few servants in charge of watching his possessions. With them in charge Stythenes, his family, and his remaining servants proceeded to the front of this ever-growing crowd. Here they sat to listen to the man on the rock. He spoke as no other man, for in him was some awesome, unseen power not of this world. All were captivated by his speech: not only by what was said, but how he said it.

This man on the rock spoke of the law as if he wrote it! He spoke of light, murder, oaths, love for enemies, prayer, fasting, judging, and a wise builder. In this man were countless ages of wisdom, though he was yet a young man. All around the people ate his words as if they were a last meal. Stythenes saw on every face true amazement. These people would be less interested if Caesar himself had stood there in front of them!

A Single Tomorrow in a Land of Yesterdays

Stythenes saw sincerity in this man, as he occasionally looked directly into his eyes. This man was relaying a message from some other place. He tried to save these people from themselves! The man on the rock concluded his teaching and proceeded through the massive crowd down the mountain. As he walked, he touched the sick, and the lame and immediately they were made whole again! Stythenes saw this and was struck dumfounded. Trying to make his way, Stythenes fought through the pressing crowd to reach this teacher of the law—this healer—but the crowd continued to press in and he was trapped!

"I have failed." Stythenes thought to himself, "The greatest man I have ever seen just passed before me, and I could not reach him."

Just then the teacher turned, and slowly proceeded towards Stythenes, healing the sick every step of the way. The healer stopped right in front of Stythenes, looking him in the eye, and whispered to him, "Don't you have a question for me, my friend."

"Where does—where does," Stythenes asked, stammering, "your great power come from, and how may I acquire knowledge of it?"

"My power comes from the Father, and you can have it only by believing in the one he has sent. You must have faith in the one he has sent, for through him is the only way to the Father!"

The healer turned away and continued down the mountainside. Stythenes long stood in wonder and amazement, thinking of what the man said. Remaining motionless, he watched the healer and the crowd slowly moving away, and finally he realized what the man meant. With desperation he shouted out for him to hear, "I do believe in you, I do! I have faith that you are the One!"

Hearing this, the healer turned to Stythenes, smiling. He then continued on his way. Stythenes thought of nothing else for days and days. He had met Jesus of Nazareth, and accepted him as Lord! All else faded to nothing, in comparison to the Holy One, so Stythenes no longer concerned himself with making a profit. Instead, Stythenes traveled with his family and freed servants, and they told all they met about Jesus Christ, the Healer and the Savior of all!

THE OLD MAN AND THE KING

~

Have you ever lived in a dream? I have. One night, as I slept fitfully, I had a very intense dream. This dream, more so than any I have ever had, was full of wrenching emotion. I felt everything as it happened; every sight and every sound was truly sensed by body, soul, and mind. It was as if my life had been transposed to another time and place. I knew every tree and hill in the landscape as if I had seen it a thousand times before. At first, I sensed that my surroundings were not real, but that feeling quickly faded as the dream world became my own.

And, as the feeling that I belonged here slowly grew, the first day in my new world began. I awoke to the smell of eggs and bacon, and sitting up disoriented I was familiar with "my" one-storey home. I dressed myself and packed a small bag for a trip. Where I was headed was unclear, but I felt urgency nonetheless. As I headed toward the kitchen, bundle over my shoulder, coming to a slightly opened door to my left, I curiously peeked through, seeing a wonderful, peaceful sight. Two young boys lay cuddled together on a cozy bed, covered by a hand-stitched quilt. These were my boys, and oddly enough I knew their names: the eldest was Daniel and the younger was Joseph. I continued on to the kitchen where I found my wife, Rachel, cooking breakfast for two.

Rachel was a pleasant woman, tall and beautiful. As I entered the room, I noticed a twinkle in her eye. I knew that I loved both her and my boys with all of my heart. Dropping my bag by the font door, giving her a hug and kiss, I took my place at the table. Rachel and I had a delightful meal together. We spoke of many things in our short time together. I thanked her for the wonderful breakfast, in the correct manner, and made my way to the boys' room to say good-bye.

Daniel and Joseph were still asleep, so I kissed them each on the forehead and whispering, "I love you," I took my leave. Back to the kitchen I went, desiring to speak with Rachel, one last time, before I left. I knew I had long trip ahead, and I found myself reluctant to leave this comfortable place. There I beheld a wondrous sight—like the rising sun—my wife was packing extra cheese, dried meat, and loaves of bread into my pack.

"You're going too break my back with such a burden, my lovely wife!" I chuckled.

"No, not too heavy for you, my strong husband!" She smiled a most beautiful smile, "Besides, I want you to return from your long journey. I have packed enough for you to linger in the city as long as your heart desires."

"I will, Rachel. I promise. Return, I mean."

With a kiss good-bye, I left my dear family to follow the path before me. The weather was just beautiful for my trek on foot. It was early autumn, and the leaves were just turning. There were shades of green, gold, red, and every color in between. In spite of the natural beauty, all that day I longed to return to my happy home, to spend the hours before twilight in the company of my wife and sons. The day slowly came to an end with a most beautiful sunset.

That night I made no campfire. I ate a light meal of bread and cheese, and lay down to find my rest for the night. Gazing at the stars, I longed, again, for the company of my wife and sons. Soon, however, I slept the night away.

The next few days were much the same. I had nearly fifty miles to travel before I reached the main road. I loved my hometown, but I did little like the long trip to the city. I would pass through several other small towns along the way. Yet I tried not to attract attention, for there were many dangerous folk about, especially during the festival season. This part of my trip took me north through mostly forested areas, with a few open fields here and there for farming.

Finally, after five uneventful days, I reached the main road, which then turned northeast into the grassy plains. Here I could make my way much faster, without the hindrance of under brush. It was nearly

A Single Tomorrow in a Land of Yesterdays

fifty more miles to the city, which was at the foot of Mount Majesty. I expected to reach the gates in five more days, and though it was still early, I decided to rest that night near the crossroads.

I lit a campfire with fallen branches I picked up along the way. There were many people passing by, most said nothing as they passed, but a few said "Hello". Just before I lay down for the night a nice, little man asked to share my fire.

"Of course. Have a seat."

"Thank you, kind sir. I am Jonathan; it is nice to meet such a kind stranger in the wild lands." He replied.

Jonathan was an excitable man, well pleased to have a warm fire to rest beside. We spoke long about his family, his first journey to the city, and how great it was to have a travel companion.

"Travel companion?" I thought, "What does he mean travel companion? I do not much desire a companion."

However, the more we spoke the more I liked his company. And I decided that I might actually enjoy finishing my trip with him. Jonathan was more of a talker than I first thought; it seemed I would have to stay up half the night just listening to his chatter. However, he soon finished and we were both sound asleep.

In the early morning, I was pulled from my sleep by the sound of Jonathan screaming. I saw him wrestling with a man twice his size. This bigger man appeared to be a thief; they were fighting over Jonathan's pack. I quickly rose to my feet only to be pummeled to the ground from behind by what was apparently a second thief. I struggled and struggled with my attacker, and finally fought free of his grasp. Striking him solidly several times in the jaw, he ran in fear and pain. I turned back to find my new friend in a heap on the ground. The man he had been struggling with won his prize, and fled. Jonathan was unconscious, but when revived seemed okay.

"Who were those men?" He asked in fear.

"They are thieves," I replied. "This land is dangerous. Always these thieves waylay travelers upon this road, but rarely so close to the crossroads. You see, warriors frequently travel this road, and thieves are no match for them. You must sleep with your valuables close at hand." I knew this was his first trip, but I did not guess he was so naïve.

"They stole my pack!" Jonathan cried in disbelief. "I can't make any money at the festival without my goods."

"I know, I know." I said, trying to console him, "but I have a deal for you. If you help me get my goods to the city to be sold, we will split the profits, half for you and half for me. Does that sound good?"

"Sounds great, friend!" He said, grabbing his jaw in pain, and forcing out a distorted smile.

So we started the next leg of our journey together, both of us protecting my pack from the burglars and thieves. In spite of his injuries, Jonathan continued at a considerable pace. I concluded he was being driven by his fear of being attacked again.

We left the road only to drink from the nearby stream, which ran off the mountain. Its water was pure and delicious, quenching our thirst completely.

Our road never ventured far from the icy stream as it wound northward toward Mount Majesty. Our travel became increasingly difficult with the crossing of the mountain's foothills. Still Jonathan was as excited as ever, and our discourse often carried us into late evening. The road was wearisome work, yet with Jonathan at my side I felt I could conquer anything. My love and care for him increased daily, and I feared the end of our journey, when we would part ways.

Along the way I decided to pick up a large walking stick, and I advised Jonathan to do the same. These staffs were not merely for leaning on; they would also aid in protecting us against thieves, which rarely used any weapon but brute force. We were now within a day's march of the city. Mount Majesty grew increasingly larger with every step, as did my fear of the growing number of travelers that surrounded us. We no longer walked alone, but continued in an ever-growing stream of life headed for the city gates, flanked on all sides by strangers.

"How do you tell the good from the bad?" asked Jonathan as he looked from side to side at our fellow travelers.

"You cannot tell by appearance." I chuckled, "How a man looks tells you nothing. What is in a man's soul either corrupts, or betters him. So unless you can see into his innermost being it is useless to

A Single Tomorrow in a Land of Yesterdays

stare." That comment I aimed at Jonathan, for he was still staring at our many unwelcome companions.

"I am sorry. But how did you know that I was not a thief?"

"I did not know about you until we started our journey together, and now I see that you are a good man." I really wanted him to understand, "You see, a far better judge of a man are his deeds than his words. Time will reveal a man's heart, and yours, my friend, is full caring and love."

As our discourse continued we neared the outer gates of the city, which faced due south. Now plain before our eyes was the city cradled by Mount Majesty, the most powerful and beautiful of all mountains. The mountain had three peaks: one to the east, one to the north, and one to the west. In between these peaks was a high plateau, which housed the mightiest of all cities. The city was walled on three sides by the mountain; it seemed as if the mountain and the city were created in one moment by a king of immeasurable power. Enemies of this city had no hope for attack. The south face of the city, the only open side, had two mighty walls to protect it. The inner wall was only slightly shorter than the outer wall, but lacked nothing in strength. The outer wall was reached by trekking down a tremendous road, which led straight from gate to gate without winding. No matter how many times seen the city, the walls, and the mountain were breathtaking.

"That's the city," Jonathan cried in amazement, "That's where the king and all his people live? I have never seen such a thing of power and glory. The king is truly a king of might. All the stories of him must be true!"

"Yes—" I longed to say something of wisdom, but I remained speechless. I had been to this city many, many times and had never given the slightest thought to the king.

Even now I could see the king's palace near the northern peak. The towering palace seemed to give off its own light as night quickly approached. The sun was disappearing in the western sky, and in the distance I could see the guards closing the giant gates of the outer wall. The gates glimmered golden in the waning light and I heard the loud report as they were flung shut. The trumpeter sounded the changing of the guard, and the procession of the mighty guardsmen, to and from the inner wall, followed.

A Single Tomorrow in a Land of Yesterdays

"Well, it looks as if we will camp outside the gates tonight," I told Jonathan, trying to be cheerful for the fear in his eyes.

"Will we meet the king tomorrow?"

"Jonathan, I must tell you, I have been to this city once a year my entire life, and I have never met the king. He is busy and I do not wish to bother him. Besides, some say that there is no king and others say that he does not care about us—any of us!"

"There must be a king! Did you not see the light from the tower? How would you explain—?"

"I would not explain it. It requires no explanation. Now, go to sleep!" I said pointing to the ground at our feet. This was the first disagreement of our friendship, and did not like the feeling it gave me.

After a few minutes I rolled over and tried to apologize, but Jonathan was already asleep. I tried and tried to get some sleep, but could not, so I got up to look around. We were at the very foot of the mountain directly facing the lower gate, which was a good half-mile up the face of the mountain; the tower near the mountain's northern peak, still glowing luminous, seemed only to brighten in the increasing darkness. To the west I could see nothing through the darkness of night. However, to the east I could see a bright flickering light, it appeared to be a great bonfire. I slowly wandered toward the light, trembling in fear. Forgetting my walking stick when I left camp, I walked on trying to stay out of the light. As I came closer, I heard faintly what sounded like wailing! Coming closer I found it was just as I heard: it sounded as if men and women were being burned alive, but their torment never ceased! I could proceed no more and I could not retreat; I was frozen. My heart raced, and I was filled with fear and dread. Somehow, I knew in my heart that whatever was happening to those people could also be my destiny.

I looked around for some ray of hope, some way out of this place. My eye fell upon the king's palace, and instantly my strength was renewed. I struggled to my feet and began to head back to Jonathan. With every step, I had to stare at the king's tower for strength because when I looked away I could not carry on, or overcome my fear. I found my way to Jonathan, who was still sleeping in peace.

A Single Tomorrow in a Land of Yesterdays

I wrestled myself into fitful sleep, with uneasy dreams of voices crying in agony for help—for relief. I dreamed of this for hours. My only peace was when my dreams led back to the light of the tower. The very thought of it warmed my soul, and yet my dreams continuously drifted back to those terrifying voices! Now I saw the people in this fire and they were calling to me to join them! And out of the fire came a terrible black beast, and it clamped its claws into my flesh, dragging me into the fire!

I awoke with a jump in a pool of sweat; Jonathan was kneeling over me shaking me and calling to me.

"I'm awake, Jonathan, I'm awake!"

"I'm sorry." Jonathan yelled, and composing himself, he said, "Thought you were dying! You were screaming in your sleep, and there was this foul voice. I don't know where it came from for there is no one else around! I thought you were burning alive for there was awful smelling smoke rising from your body! I am sorry, I'm so sorry!"

Jonathan then recoiled in fear, looking directly behind me. I quickly rolled, grabbed my stick, and stood defensively only to be knocked squarely to the ground. I again stood and assailed my attacker with a barrage from my stick. However, I was no match for my enemy, this time he struck me with unbelievable force and all went black!

Soon afterward I came to. I was facing the lower gate, and I saw two of the city guards running with all speed towards us. I struggled to get up when, WHAM, all went black again!

This time my awakening was much more pleasant. Jonathan and I were side by side in a giant, soft bed. All around us was the soft glow and warmth of light. It seemed we were in a room in a high tower for there was a balcony to our right overlooking the city. A man was standing over us to our left. This was a man of power like none ever seen. He seemed to us to be as tall as a tree, though much more powerful. On his head was a crown with many jewels, and he was adorned with a pure white robe, which emanated a warm, white light that filled the room. His hands were stronger than wrought iron and yet gentle as a morning breeze. He placed one hand on each of our heads, and all pain, all bruises, and all sorrows faded to nothing.

A Single Tomorrow in a Land of Yesterdays

As he removed his hands from us he smiled and said, in a clear fluid voice, "I am Heishua, the King's son. He has sent me here to care for you, and now that you are well, he asked me to invite you to the table for a royal feast. He has given you much already, but will gladly give you more if only you ask. So come now, if you will, into my father's presence. Follow me, I will lead you there."

Heishua's voice was soothing yet powerful, like a great and mighty river. And without hesitation, Jonathan and I were on his heels following his every step as we wound ever downward to the King's table. We passed many a room with beds just like ours. Every detail in the palace was perfect in every way. Silver and gold were used as if it was as easy to come by as wood. I began to notice that everything was spotless and beautiful except for Jonathan and I. We were still wearing our dirty traveling clothes.

"I am sorry, Heishua, your Highness, but should we not change our clothes before we meet the King?" I humbly asked.

"That is not necessary, for all is changed in the King's presence. You can do nothing to make yourselves ready to meet the King. All you must do is choose to, or not to, accept him as your King. He will not force himself on you. You have the choice to leave his presence anytime you wish, but I would not if I were you!"

"We could never wish that!" Said Jonathan looking first to Heishua, then to me. He seemed to be asking me for reassurance.

"No. Never!" I agreed.

Just then Heishua stopped in a marvelous, golden archway and stretched out his mighty arm. We entered, under his powerful reach, into a grand banquet hall. Its ceilings, unsupported and arched, were at least four stories high. Everything was trimmed in gold and emitted a powerful glow. Right there before us was the table; it stretched on and on, for what seemed like miles. Around it sat thousands of men and women, great and small. At the head of this enormous table sat the King. I could not make out his countenance because of the glow coming from his very presence. I then realized that he and his son were the very source of this all-consuming light!

The King silenced the entire crowd and welcomed us into his presence. His voice seemed to control all things. Quickly we were surrounded by servants and rushed to the King's side, where instantly our clothing was washed clean and white by his great power and light. We both bowed our knees to show our gratitude and allegiance. It seemed that we owed this great King our very lives. In his presence all else became insignificant.

The King himself picked us both up in his great arms sitting us at his side for the banquet.

"Let all the city rejoice, for today I have two more sons. Let us all be merry, for my lost children have come home to their father. Let us celebrate and be glad! Let all the city rejoice!" Said the King in a mighty, booming voice. The King's servants, in turn, echoed this, throughout the entire city. It was carried all the way to the outer gate.

There at the King's side we ate and drank for what seemed like days. It was as if time had no meaning here in the King's Banquet Hall. Before too long, Jonathan and I, desired to go tell everyone we knew about this great King and his generosity. I longed to have my family by my side at this great feast.

"Mighty Lord and King, it is my desire to go and tell everyone about you," I exclaimed, "Please, King, give Jonathan and I leave to bring all we can to your presence."

"It is also my desire that you do this," came his powerful reply. "It is my desire that all should come and live in my presence. Go and bring back all that you can, for I long to make them my children. They must have faith that I exist, and that I can save them from their troubles as I have done for you. I will send my son with you, though he will not go as the Prince of Power. Follow my son, for he knows the way better than you, and listen to his every word. There are many perils on your road, though with my son you shall not be in danger. Remember me, that you will not be deceived. Take this book that I have written for my children so you can convince your friends and family to come back to their true King! Take my love and the love of my son with you, and do not forget these words I have spoken. I have put my blessing upon you because of your willingness to serve. Do not forget whom you serve! Now go with my blessing!"

In a matter of hours we were prepared for our journey. The King had prepared the way for us. We were met at the inner gate by a large cart, filled every kind of supply, pulled by a team of horses to help us on our journey. After we thanked the King for his many blessings Jonathan and I jumped on the cart and headed down the road for the outer gate. Along with us came Heishua, no longer dressed as prince, but as a common man. Although he was unadorned, his power could not be completely suppressed, and he still glowed of that marvelous light.

The captain of the guardsmen and two of his mighty men escorted us to the outer gate. We came, at last, to the foot of the mountain and turned east. I thought back to the night before we entered the great city and fear gripped me again. Even though it was now daylight I could still see the inferno up ahead. A smoke was rising from the fire; fear and dread seized my companion and I.

Heishua urged us onward, "Do not fear, with me by your side no harm will come to you. Don't you hear those voices in torment? Would you leave them to be destroyed? Come, we must help them!"

With that we pressed on, getting ever closer to the source of this evil, which we could now feel permeate our hearts. We traveled on through a strange darkness even though it was midday. We came to a structure atop a small hill. With just three walls, it was open to the front where the path met it. Behind the back wall there rose a terrible plume of smoke and ash. People were coming from every direction to this place seemingly unaware of the evil. In the middle of the structure a crowd was gathered. Heishua compelled us to move forward into the crowd, where he stood behind us with hands on our shoulders, keeping us calm and clear.

We were utterly amazed at what we saw there: An old man, if that is what it was, stood behind a table peddling as if at a market, but this was no market! Behind the man was a door that presumably led to the source of the smoke, but it was closed, barring our sight. On this old man's table were piles of junk; literally it was stacked with garbage. He was giving an intriguing sales pitch, and people were giving everything they had to get a piece of this refuse! Some were even coming back for seconds, and thirds, and so on. These people were going crazy about this trash. They would proudly show their friends what they had bought, not realizing that everything there was worthless! It was entirely repulsive. I could not understand what was making these people so crazy, and just then I caught the old man's eye!

He gazed deeply into my soul as he told me how much I needed his next sale piece, telling me how much better my life would be with this piece of trash. I tried to break eye contact, but I was enticed by his fluid voice and his way with words. I continued to listen. He never slowed down, paused, or wavered in his tactics.

With every word my vision was changed into what he was trying to tell me. This place of darkness and evil was transformed before my eyes into a place of light, and good! I was buying into his speech and was about to respond when Jonathan slapped me, breaking my gaze, and bringing back reality.

"Come out of it," he begged, "look what is happening to those people!"

I looked, and saw, that those customers who continued to come back for more were eventually chained up. They were not only chained up, but they were dragged back through that one doorway by these huge black beasts. These beasts were just like the creature I saw in my nightmare! There through a tiny opening in the door I could see these people being dragged to the edge of the inferno and cast in. As the beasts threw in one person they would come back and grab another only to repeat this process over and over again!

Once again I was caught in the eye of the old man. He continued to work on me trying to convince me of the beauty of his trash. Jonathan was unaware that I had fallen under the old man's spell. The old man convinced me to forget everything I had seen in the King's palace, and all my cares for friends and family were sent to the back of my mind. I no longer felt like a King's son, I felt like a child without control! I found myself running forward, shouting every step of the way!

"Give it to me," I commanded, "give it to me! I need it! I have no money, but I will give everything I have. Take all you want! Just give it to me!"

With that, a smile came to the old man's face, and I saw his true, evil nature exposed in his forked tongue. "Take him away, and feed him to the flames. He belongs to me! Destroy him! I want to see him in eternal torment!"

Then two of his horrible beasts jumped on me, and there I lay in their arms, a ruined piece of flesh. Blood was gushing from where their claws pierced my skin. They hauled me to the door; I was helpless in their crushing grip! And before me arose my destruction—a writhing mass of men in the very midst of the flame; I was to become one of them! The stench filled my nostrils, and I could no longer breathe. Why have I come here? I looked down, seeing myself still clutching that piece of refuse for which I had given everything. I dropped it immediately, and screamed for help!

"Heishua, Heishua," I cried out, "I'm sorry, I'm so sorry! Please take me back! I'm sorry I forgot you! Please, take me back! Save me, you are my Lord! Forgive me, I pray!"

Without hesitation Heishua stepped forward and commanded that the old man free me. "Let them go," he said, "all of them. I will take their place, and I will pay their price. Let them go, now! Let their eyes be opened!"

I was dropped immediately and I began to crawl back toward Jonathan. Once again I could see the reality of the situation and was happy to be free, but I remembered the words of Heishua. I did not want him to pay for my mistakes.

"No, no!" I exclaimed, "I cannot let you pay my price"

Heishua grabbed me, and my scars vanished. Then he looked me in the eyes, with no faltering in his voice and said, "It is the only way, you will see. I will open everyone's eyes and set them free. If they claim me, then I will claim them. I will come back; trust me. I will pay the price for all!"

With that, he was beaten by those nasty black creatures. Not because of their power did they beat him, but because he allowed them to. He had to pay the penalty for all, through pain. They continued to beat Heishua as they dragged him toward the door; his body was a bleeding, broken mass of pain and torment. All Jonathan and I could do was watch in complete horror! The beasts threw our Prince into the flames and began to rejoice. For they believed they had destroyed the Prince of Power. Jonathan and I were confused—bewildered—not knowing what to do. When suddenly there came a blinding flash that destroyed all darkness in its path. The three walls were flattened and the fire was quenched. The old man and his beasts were scattered abroad, and in the midst of their victory their kingdom was destroyed! For there arose the Prince of Power, and all power of darkness was destroyed. Heishua climbed to the top of that small hill; the keys to all chains were in his hands, and at his feet everyone bowed. Now all eyes saw him as the Lord of Glory!

" Now arise, my children, go to the city and claim the King as your king!" he said this to the entire crowd on that desolate hill. "Bring as many as you can to join in the feast at the King's table!"

Every person on that hill scrambled to do just what he said, except for Jonathan and I. There we stood at his feet to see if he would still come with us.

"I will be with you in spirit and in truth. Do not forget my words, and you will have a safe journey. Now go, and hurry. Bring back as many as you can, for time is running out!"

So on our cart we raced off to tell friends and family all about this Lord of Glory, the Mighty King, and the Prince of Power. We brought with us as many as would come, and it was a great procession of the King's returned children. All were welcomed by the King, no matter what they had done in life. There at the King's table were perfect peace and harmony, for all!

At this point I awoke from my dream—a dream lived, yet only dreamed—and thanked God the father, and Jesus Christ his son, for all they had done, and will do, for me. We do owe our lives to God, and we do have forgiveness of sins through his son, Jesus.

STRANGE COMFORT

~

Dust was everywhere, or more precisely, nearly everywhere, upon that tattered wooden floor. Dust had always been a nuisance in my great-grandfather's mountain cabin—a beautiful cabin, in the perfect location—atop the highest peak in the range. As far back as I could remember we were forced to clean the dust during our periodic visits, but this dust was no ordinary accumulation; it was more on the line of bizarre, and, not to mention, very strangely dispersed. For towards the center of the main chamber there was a distinct path, as if something had been dragged into the adjacent bedroom disturbing this prodigiously thick layer of dust, and leaving behind a thinner layer. All the strange sights I saw in a matter of only a few seconds were enough to concern me, but what I was about to discover in the next few hours was enough to terrify me for the remainder of my life!

This cabin was in no way the same condition I had left it, almost ten months earlier. As I walked through the already open entry door, my senses were overloaded with all I saw, smelled, and touched. My normally very orderly cabin had been completely ransacked. Every piece of furniture was stacked as if for the purpose of blocking all windows and doors—every single entry point, including the chimney, was barricaded! My mind raced and my heart pounded—a paralyzing fear gripped my body to the bone! With the strength that remained in my form, I quickly surveyed the calamity at hand.

From my point of view—still as a stone—facing west through the eastern door, I took in every detail I could manage. The place was in complete disarray, and the reek of death was sickening! Dishes were

A Single Tomorrow in a Land of Yesterdays

scattered all around with books, pots and pans, toiletries, blankets, tools, and lamps; nearly all the cabinet doors had been torn from the hinges, and those that remained attached were hanging loosely, ready to fall. It seemed to me that some great struggle took place in my dear cabin; the signs were everywhere, including some very deep scratches in various wooden items throughout the entire area of my perception. To convey the feeling of fear that I now endured is beyond words! Everything that I noticed only deepened—intensified remarkably—fear's hold upon my once intrepid constitution.

It appeared that the doorway in which I stood was to be the last entry barricaded. To my left, lying on the floor, were a disheveled stack of lumber, some nails, and a large hammer. The evidence was clear enough; someone was trying to keep something out! This was too much for me. I madly raced about the main room looking high and low for the double-barrel shotgun, which, like everything else, was missing from its usual place above the mantle. Eventually I found it, and I will explain where, but first I must point out an observation that I have foregone because of its extreme peculiarity.

As I mentioned earlier, this incredibly thick dust covered the entire cabin floor, except a strange circle—strange is a gross understatement. This circle, near the middle of the main chamber, was some four feet in diameter, and was, as far as I could tell perfect in all manners. In the center of this anomaly, as it were, was an upended coffee table, which appeared to be resting unevenly on top of some object. Fearing the worst, I turned it over by kicking the legs and was greatly relieved, yet perplexed, with what I found—a Bible, and my great-grandfather's Remington double-barrel shotgun!

Before this time, it had been clear to me that someone had stayed in my cabin without my welcome. However, finding a Bible lying open, with the barrels of the gun lying diagonally across the crinkled pages—it appeared the gun was dropped or thrown down—was enough to imagine the most horrific scenario! What had happened here? Why was my 'guest' sitting upon the floor holding my shotgun, and reading from the Holy Bible?

Answers to these questions, and more, I would soon discover, but for now all I could do was speculate. Obviously the barricaded entries, as well as the shotgun, were for protection, but from what?

The Bible, I assumed, had been for comfort, strength, or something like that; personally, I had very little faith, and the Bible brought no comfort to my already frayed nerves.

It now became all too clear that whatever had happened could still be happening, and whomever had been here could still be here! In a flash, I picked up the gun, and opening the breach, found that both barrels had been fired—two shells sprang empty to the floor. This only intensified my need for protection. Rummaging around on the cluttered floor, I quickly found a nice pocketful of unused shells—maybe six or seven—and then set my mind to the task of securing the four rooms that were now hidden behind closed doors! A nauseating feeling crept steadily into my body. I thought that I had previously comprehended the term 'sensory overload', but I realized that I was clueless—until now!

I had already seen the entirety of the main chamber, which housed the living and dining areas, as well as the kitchen. The master bedroom and the bathroom were connected to this main room: the latter by way of the western wall, and the former by way of the southern wall. The stairs to the loft were next to the northern wall, and landed on an open platform to the east, in such a way that from the main chamber the two doors for the upper rooms could be easily seen—both were closed. My search would start in the loft, then proceed to the bathroom, and finish in the master bedroom, where I could lock the door, and gather my self together; thus was my plan.

With the shotgun breach open, I began to slowly climb the stairs, loading it as I went—one shell, then two. I was ready for whatever might happen. Approaching the landing, my limbs grew heavier with each step, and my throat began to burn—the nausea only intensified! I reached the top, and found the dust to be considerably lighter and the dread fear retreat a little.

Reaching the first door and preparing to open it was much easier than I anticipated. With a twist of the knob I threw it open; to my surprise, it was in much the same order as I had left it. Leaving nothing to chance, I looked everywhere for some shred of evidence, but only found that room completely empty. One door down, and three to go!

A Single Tomorrow in a Land of Yesterdays

With finding the first room in pleasant order, opening the next door was much easier to master. It proceeded much the same as the first room, with only a slight change: it was clear that this room had been trespassed. This room was a bedroom, and the bed had obviously been used. The blankets and sheets were pulled back, and other things were not as I had left them. Through the window above the bed I could see the sun begin sinking. The shadows lengthened, as the natural light in the cabin would soon be gone. With this revelation, the previously residing fear crept back stealthily into my soul! Otherwise, this room was also empty. Two doors down, and two to go!

So, I continued with my search plan. To the stairs I rushed, when, once again, the smell of death smacked me cold! It filled my nostrils, and reached, it seemed, to my very soul. Nevertheless, I slowly crept down the stairs, shotgun to shoulder, and closer to my next horrible discovery. On the floor in front of the bottom stair was not a single print—a print in the dust that was not mine, nor was it there when I came up the stairs! The fact that there was a print was not the worst part of the discovery. It was like nothing I had ever seen, with five toes, or fingers, in front, and two opposable ones behind! Whatever had made the print was beyond me. Was it reptile, bird, or something more horrible? How did it get there? Why only one?

My thoughts raced wildly as I proceeded with my plan; the third door stood dauntingly before me, as if mocking my absolute terror. Opening it timidly, I stepped back and brought the gun to my shoulder—both barrels ready! To my relief, nothing jumped out; however, the bathroom was smashed similarly to the main room. The large oval mirror had been broken, with the glass partly in the sink, and partly still on the wall. As I quickly checked the rest of the room—all clear—I noticed blood spattered here and there with the scattered mirror glass! It seemed that my 'guest' had struck the mirror, and his blood intermixed with the glass. This, however, did in no way explain the print discovery, though I felt I would figure it out all to soon.

Moving closer to the mirror to examine it, I noticed my face, as I had never seen it before. It wore upon it great fear, and the foreboding of doom! As I gazed at my face like a stranger, with bulging, red eyes, I saw something behind me, in the main chamber, move! Quickly I wheeled around and raced into the dining area—nothing there, nothing anywhere in the main room! My faith in the unseen had grown dramatically. After all, it seemed that shadows move, and it was evident they had seven toes! It was crazy, or I was! Three doors down, and one to go!

Fear now controlled my every muscle, and every step seemed an hour, at best, as I approached the last door. This door I opened the easiest possible way—clearing both barrels of the shotgun! Quickly I reloaded, as it swung wide, and remembered the irregular path in the dust led into this room. Just when I thought my horror was at its limits, it was again stretched to a higher degree! I had, apparently, discovered the source of the reek! The smell of death emanated from this place! The upper half of a bare skeleton lay at the end of the bed! Its bare arms grasped the bed frame, and it faced me with wide-open jaws, as if screaming! Now fear gripped me entirely, melting my once steadfast heart! The look of horror upon the carcass was surely not as reviling as my own.

At this time I could foresee nothing worse. This was, after all, apparently my 'guest', and this meant his attempt at self-defense failed—miserably! I felt I would swoon, so quickly I knelt to avoid the obviously disastrous end of falling unconscious. As my knees hit hard on the floor, my eyes remained stuck on the bones of my 'guest', and I noticed something run out from underneath the bed! I would give this thing no time for questioning, as it ran straight for the door directly in front of me. A combined blast from both barrels stopped it dead! What was it? Only a rat, and not the source of the print! At that moment many things happened: the skeleton shattered into a pile of ashes on the floor, I heard a great clawing and scratching on the floor behind me, and for a brief moment I fell unconscious.

I awoke, which seemed a miracle in itself, to find the cabin growing dark. The sun must have been setting. I sprang up with as much vigor as I could possibly muster, grabbed the gun, reloaded it, and remembering the clawing sound wheeled to face it! There was no beast staring at me, nor was it breathing its hot breath upon me. However, outside the bare circle on the floor was scrawled, in deep hideous scratches, a message which read: **YOU'RE NEXT!**

In the center of the circle the Bible remained, undaunted by whatever evil was resident here! I rushed to it, seeking: strength, reassurance, courage, peace, or whatever else it might offer. I began reading whatever I could, and in spite of the circumstance it began to subside my fear! Many things I read, frantically, and many things I learned, in the dissipating light. I read, and I read, afraid to look up from the words; they did truly comfort me. In the front of this Bible were two references, inscribed repeatedly. These two verses I looked up, and read aloud. The very words revived my frightful soul:

"Everyone who calls on the name of the Lord will be saved." (Acts 2:21), and *"Submit yourselves, then, to God. Resist the devil, and he will flee."* (James 4:7).

Just then, it became ominously apparent to me, that here I was sitting in this circle while holding this Bible and shotgun, just as my predecessor! I was now in the same situation as he had been, and now he is a pile of ashes on the bedroom floor! What was now my fate? I knew, now, that God was with me, never to forsake me. Be this thing biological beast, or Satan himself, I would not be alone. My mind began drifting, as I gazed on the ashes that were once a man—a man in my situation—and I wondered what he was like, what he believed in, and why he was destroyed in this manner? With these thoughts heavy in my mind the sun set, and with my fear rising again the light of the full moon shone through the picture window by the entry door, falling lightly around me.

The moonlight—I thought my friend—revealed my next source of dismay. On the floor about two feet ahead of me was, again, a single print! Thoughts of horror and death filled my mind to capacity; no room was left for logic, or self-preservation! Leaning forward to closer examine this print brought the greatest fright yet! Upon my leaning forward, I bumped into an unseen obstacle—covered by shadow and long hair! Jumping back, out of my precious circle, and firing both barrels in the direction of my enemy, I revealed his entire hidden form by the light of the blast! Surely in Heaven and Earth there is no form as hideous as the one that now stared directly into my face—directly through my face, and into my empty soul! My life was now hopelessly in the hands of the One who hates all!

Now this enemy of mine took physical shape—misshaped shape! As I lay upon the floor, convulsing and weeping in fear, he towered over my tiny helpless form, threatening me in silence! Every second seemed an hour, and without thought I perceived every detail of this haunting 'devil'. All his anti-luminous body—a body somewhat reptile, somewhat lion—was covered in a hair unlike any other. It was a fine hair, long and black, and it was a powerful form that reached down its clawed hand, picking up my nearly lifeless form. Now I was face to face with it! Somehow, my eyes would not close; I was forced to look, and be afraid!

A smile came to his face that shook my soul, exposing two rows of long jagged teeth, and it seemed he would swallow me whole! My body was given a beating that no human should have to endure as I was thrown around the cabin like a child's toy. My blood was spattered on the walls, ceiling, and floors; it was pouring from me in tremendous amounts! The only sound waves that struck my ears were those of my bones being shattered, as glass. I knew that I should no longer be living, but somehow I remained alive—alive for his pleasure!

For what seemed like hours, I was tossed painfully here and there. And now that he ceased my physical torment, it seemed he would torment my soul; I became aware of his shrieking laughter! This laughter pierced me deeper than the wounds my body now held, and then the most horrible feeling came upon me! I felt him reach through my body, grasping my eternal soul. Feeling a heat like the flames of Hell, he began tearing into me! How could this be happening?

With a grip that would splinter stone, he held my soul, and began to pull it from my body! He was, obviously, on his way back to Hell, intending to take me with him. I now realized what destroyed my cabin, and made the path on the dusty floor. For I was now making similar paths, as he attempted to split me—body from soul! Passing near the Bible as he dragged me on, I suddenly remembered what I had learned, and strength entered my soul that I had never before felt. It freed my frozen lips!

"You will not have me." I shouted in command, "I call upon the name of Jesus, my Lord, to save me." A light encompassed my body as I continued, "And now I resist you, Satan, by the Power and Blood of Jesus! Flee now, my Enemy! You cannot—you will not have me!"

In a single instant my enemy had left, whimpering as he went! But what will become of me? Could I possibly recover from my physical trauma? These answers I do not know, but now I know what will happen in the END!

THIRTEEN

~

It is upon the brink of death we often discover the true nature of our constitution. For myself, the fact that I am not invincible nearly shattered my existence, and to this day, many years later, this near-death experience still haunts my dreams. As a cold shadow that covers my heart, it continues to breathe its icy breath upon my soul. Recounting to you this event—this life-changing event—still sends the sharpest chill up my spine, despite the lapse of time!

It had been one of the coldest Januarys on record, and I, as usual, was out alone that fateful night returning home from a little secluded jaunt of snowmobile riding and ice fishing. Winter was always bitter around my home—a fact of life that one becomes accustom to—in Michigan's upper peninsula. So, pulling my snowmobile behind my pickup, with a lonely, snowy road in front of me, I started home a couple of hours after dusk. With the heater blasting and the radio up I began the forty-mile drive into what started as light snow.

Being miles from civilization was something that I had always cherished; I could leave my responsibilities of work and home far behind, letting it all loose in the wild! My wife was very understanding—at times too understanding—it almost seemed she wanted me to go away. I always went, but this time it felt different. When I told her that I was going away for a few hours she tensed up, and for nearly the first time asked me—no, begged me—to stay home. Without a good reason to stay, I told her I would be home in a few hours. Simply informing me that it was "cold" was not enough, so I kissed her goodbye and walked out the door!

A Single Tomorrow in a Land of Yesterdays

Her behavior, or "concern" as she called it, really began to trouble my thoughts while the snow picked up! It was now coming down in huge white flakes, impeding my vision and sense of direction. With every mile it became more difficult to see the road, slowing my progress to a mere thirty-five miles per hour! A sense of foreboding overshadowed my every thought. I strained my eyes peering into the white blur, trying to detect anything ahead. Knowing my wife was waiting, and probably, becoming more hysterical with every minute, I continually asked God to get me home safely—to the love of my life!

Turning off the radio, I devoted every ounce of concentration to seeing my way through the snowfall! The anxiety was overwhelming, but to my delight I actually met some oncoming traffic; two cars and a pickup slowly passed in the opposite direction. My heart lifted and my muscles relaxed. I was not the only crazy person out tonight! All my concern and worry were for nothing, or were they?

Without warning, there appeared in front of me a large dark object, roughly the size of a man, concealed in shadow! All was a blur, except one thing: I know, without doubt, that I saw two eyes glaring back at me! Without thought or hesitation, I cut the wheel to avoid striking the person, animal, or whatever it was! As I slid out of control, I clearly saw "it" remain perfectly still; the eyes I could still see, almost mocking me! Although I was familiar with driving on slick roads, this was too much too fast. Sliding sideways, I instinctively counter-steered, unfortunately over-correcting my slide and the truck slid the other way! It was too much; my heart would soon explode! The snowmobile trailer crashed into the bed, and the truck slid off the road to the top of an embankment! For a brief moment, I saw my coming misfortune. The headlights of the pickup shone to the bottom of the embankment, probably thirty feet down! Just a split second of hope that the sliding would stop before the tumble began!

It seemed the rolling would never stop! I just knew I would never see my lovely wife again. I flew this way and that, cut or bruised by everything I thrashed against. The truck eventually came to rest, as did the snowmobile and trailer. So, there I was hanging by the seatbelt in the crushed cab of my truck, overturned in the snow—a bloody, bruised mess! Immediately I thanked the Lord for allowing me to live through it, without a single broken bone, and asked Him for strength to make it home! I knew that I was still at least twenty miles from home, and some twelve miles from the nearest town! How would I make it home in this condition—through twelve miles of snow and bitter cold?

With these thoughts heavy on my mind, I attempted to free myself from the seatbelt. I lost all sense of time while struggling to get free. With the realization that I would not be freed so easily, I began checking my wounds. All seemed okay, that is, nothing seemed to require major medical attention, though blood flowed fairly freely! With the blood flowing to my head, my mind began to cloud, when I remembered that I had a way out. I always carried a pocketknife, and this horrible night was no exception!

Free of the belt, I struggled to crawl through the mangled doors— to no avail! I had just paused my struggle, when I became aware of a terrifying sound! I faintly heard, straining to hear it, the most demented chuckling I could imagine! And as I lay there, paralyzed with fear, it rose to a demoniacal laughter—only the beginning of my horror. Peering through the window I had just struggled to crawl out of, I saw the snow quit, and the moon come out, casting an evil shadow toward my truck! Now, to accompany the tormenting sound, was a shadow to torture my thoughts! I saw the source of the eyes on the road, and the cause of my wreck!

I realized that someone had intentionally caused me to crash, and it seemed he, for it was a man's laughter, had found the result quite enjoyable! Fearing to be heard, I dared not move, as the laughter came ever nearer. The man kicked the side of my truck and made his way back up the embankment. As he walked away I heard him say in his possessed voice, "I'll be back for you tomorrow." Apparently, I could anxiously await his return tomorrow, or I could leave my truck and head for safety. However difficult the path might be, the choice was not!

By the light of the moon I crawled from my truck, making my way to the snowmobile. I quickly found it missing from the overturned trailer. After a few moments of struggling about in the darkness, I discovered the battered sled upright and nearly covered with

A Single Tomorrow in a Land of Yesterdays

snow. As quickly as possible I had it started, and grabbing my gear raced it up toward the road, for home.

If this had been the end of my misfortune, I could then tell this story with a smiling face, but in reality things grew steadily worse. I must tell the remainder of this tale with a heavy, dread-filled heart. I can barely form the words with my quivering lips! I made it merely two miles before my sled broke down—engine seized! Not far, on the opposite side of the road, I saw the tracks of another snowmobile. This should have worried me little; after all, while I was out I had seen many tracks besides my own. Yet for some unknown reason, I just knew these were the tracks of the owner of those hideous eyes!

After much consideration, I decided to follow, from a distance. For hours I trudged along, as best I could, in snow nearly two feet deep. All the while, my time was spent in the futile task of covering my own tracks while not becoming too conspicuous to the tracks I followed. Eventually the tracks led off the road into a narrow, ominous lane much over grown with shrubs and small trees, surrounded by dense woods. It appeared to have been a driveway, but it was now a tight fit for even the smallest of automobiles!

To add to my fear, I realized the sun was rising—it was now morning—and the "eyes" would soon return to my crash site! Every crack and rustle of the branches above caused my heart to skip a beat. I proceeded following the tracks, much slower than before, ducking from tree to tree. Keeping the lane far to my left I continued on, forming a plan in my head.

If this were the home of the crazy-eyed man, than I would wait for him to leave and call the police with his phone. With all things considered, I knew this was a horrible plan, and it gave me little comfort! Nevertheless, I would proceed, knowing that remaining still would definitely be my end.

In the distance, not more than a half mile, I heard a sled roar to life, racing down the lane—in my direction! It was him—same eyes, same burly shadow of a man! No sooner had he disappeared than I took off running down the lane toward his house. No longer concerned about leaving tracks, I desperately ran toward that house with all might and desperation, neglecting any precautions. The hope of returning home to my wife was now in sight, or was it?

A Single Tomorrow in a Land of Yesterdays

The house, very large and intricately ornamented, appeared as if a shadow of the past hung heavily over it. It must have been beautiful in its time, but it now looked hopelessly out of place in this twenty-first century. Drawing my knife, I reached the front door, feeling a sudden heaviness come over me. As if I stepped on the threshold of an ancient world, the colors of my clothes and skin faded. I now blended into the cold, gray, almost black-and-white feel of this house, and I shuddered in fear as I opened the great creaking door of this cavernous abode!

In complete stealth, from door to door, I searched desperately for a phone. I became aware of the sound of music and a dim, flickering light near the back of the first floor, so without thought I approached. Carefully peering around the opening, to what appeared to be a dining room, I discovered the sources of light and sound! The clear sound of music came from an antique phonograph. In an extravagant fireplace there raged a wonderful warm fire, giving light to the entire room and the most horrible revelation!

There, seated around a large table, were twelve corpses, arranged in the act of a family meal! From what I could gather there was a 'mother' at the foot, and eleven children, varying in age, arranged in hideous formation around the table. Two seats remained empty: the head, and one adjacent to it. I understood from this sight, that I was meant to be one of these posed corpses—to join this meal of the dead—number thirteen!

Shrinking from this horror, I discovered an antique phone on the wall, in the expansive hallway. To my dismay, I heard no dial tone, only the sound of an approaching snowmobile, through my opposite ear! *He* was already coming back and had obviously seen my tracks outside his house! My end would come soon—never to feel the warmth, and love, of my wife again—and I would be placed in the seat next to the head, in this never-ending meal of flesh and bone 'mannequins'!

I madly raced about putting to action a plan—a hopeless plan—that my incoherent mind feebly put together! I swapped clothes with one corpse, roughly my stature, and hid his body in the adjacent room, taking his place at the dinner table. Stripping that ghastly corpse and dressing myself in his smelly clothes would haunt my memory forever! Praying to God for safety and looking at the posed corpses around me, I assumed the position of the removed corpse as best I could remember. The look of these 'mannequins' was reviling; the firelight almost brought their stone cold features to life!

No sooner had I taken position and with all my strength calmed my breathing, than the front door swung open and slammed shut! I now heard footsteps running down the hall directly to this dining room! I dared not move, nor breathe. He knew I was there, but he seemed uncertain where. My plan was working, but now what? I could not hold my breath forever!

I heard him panting heavily from his recent run, as he made his way past the head of the table toward the fireplace. Then he began in a slow, but extremely powerful voice, "Madeline," he said. Evidently *Madeline* was the corpse that assumed the foot of the table. "Where did thirteen go? I know he is here, though not in his rightful place." His voice grew to a frantic pace, taunting my silence.

I had to breathe while his back was turned and involuntarily sighed. He made no response, except he leaned on the wall beside the fireplace, grabbing some unseen object. Never did I move from my pose, nor did I shake, but a growing sense told me that he knew where I was! My heart raced, yet I did not move. Nothing in my life could have ever prepared me for what was about to take place!

He turned, carrying what looked like an axe, and walked toward me repeating, "Where is thirteen, where is thirteen?" again and again! I made no motion, thinking my heart had been paralyzed with the same fear that gripped my bones. Losing all sense of time—all sense whatsoever—I became lost in a world of fear! He stopped behind me. What was he doing? Was he raising the axe? This would be my end, and it almost seemed refreshing to know my horror would soon be over. Though my heart longed to see, just once more, all the things I hold dear: friends, family, and my beloved wife.

With a sudden, blinding jerk his deadly axe-stroke fell! Hope remained, though not much, for his stroke fell deep within the corpse next to me. I heard the crunch of breaking bones, and while he struggled to free his axe from its victim I arose. It seemed that I surprised him as much as he did me, but I was the first to strike. While he still gripped the axe I kicked him with all my might to the ground.

Wasting no time, I jumped on him, drew my trusty pocketknife, and buried it deep within his throat! With that thrust of mine, his wild eyes nearly burst from their sockets! Never have I seen something so horribly gruesome.

I remember very little about my feelings at that moment, but it seemed I had the upper hand. Blood shot from the wound with every pulse of his heart. I, however, would not linger to make sure of his demise, and with his warm blood all over my hands I left his twitching body, racing for my freedom! I moved with fury to his still running sled, not letting go of the throttle until I reached the nearest town.

As I said, we do not truly know our own constitution until we stand upon the brink of death! I am satisfied to discover no more about the profound mystery of my constitution, much less the mystery of just what happened there. For, you see, after telling the police the entire tale, wearing the smelly, antique clothes of a dead man, I do not know just what happened in that time forsaken house! The police sent an investigator to that location and found nothing but a puddle of blood, and my clothes! Needless to say, I have never, and will never, return to that area!

Now, snowy winter nights are nightmares for me. I am haunted by the memory of the wild-eyed father, and his family of corpses! When big snowflakes fall I wonder where they are now, and who will be "thirteen"?

THE VALLEY

~

More than mere hills as the name suggests the High Hills were, from birth, my home. These 'hills' were a great mountain range along the western coast of a great empire. And though the world has changed immensely and my own eyes have seen the darkness, their beauty remains unaltered. From the snow-capped peaks in the north (Mount Veritheo being the pride thereof), to the southern foothills, the High Hills will ever be unspoiled by human activities.

I had built a life upon the peaks of these mountains, coming to know them as well as any man could, having traveled ceaselessly among the cities scattered throughout the numerous plateaus. It was a lovely dwelling, and a lovely life, built with the fabric of the mountainside and nestled in a lower plateau, overlooking the sea to the west. Though now it is nothing more than a distant, faint memory—a clouded, vague memory—covered by inscrutable mist that now overshadows my heart! I no longer recall the sound of waves crashing upon the sandy shores, nor the smell of salty seas intertwining the scent of fresh apples from the orchard, and least of all, the comfort of returning home after long journeys!

No! All that has been taken—stolen—from me, supplanted with despair. Now in this accursed place, looking down at the blood dripping from my hands, I wonder if it were even possible to find home again, or the self I thought I knew! But I must tell of how I came here (having yet to explain where 'here' is), and how this shadow, like cancer, diseased my life!

I had ventured nearly a fortnight deep into the mountains north and east of my home, intending to build a store of meat for the

A Single Tomorrow in a Land of Yesterdays

approaching winter; meat vanishes as the snow rises. Fortune had abandoned me. The weather turned ill, chill and drizzle became my incessant, loathsome companions only a week into my journey. With every stride thoughts of home—dry and warm, roaring fires upon the hearth—consumed me. An ambivalent fate awaited me as I trudged upon mud and stone, through thicket and glade. Knowing the dire strait of a hungry winter I plodded on with hood and cloak drawn tight, and determination sternly upon my face.

It had been two long days since I last fit arrow to string, and my kill was one mere mountain fowl. My entire journey to date had rendered that fowl, and two of the same the very day I set forth. On the fourteenth day my heart lightened, and with the discovery of tracks left by a great hart, hope rekindled. The trail was fresh and deep in the mud, easily followed as it led toward the edge of a wide bowl-shaped vale.

The vale was beautiful, yet treacherous, to behold. For the inner parts contained a rich forest, scattered with glades, and the wondrously wide and swift Canyon River, emptying into the ocean, yet its treachery was its sheer outer walls! The vale was wholly surrounded, except where the river ran through its canyon, by looming vertical walls of cold, unfriendly stone. I had seen this valley before, wishing to never encounter it again, and I had ever avoided the verge for fear of a single misstep; now, I came nearer with every step in pursuit of my prey. And there he stood: the proudest, most noble, hart ever seen by man—upon the very brink!

I struggled on in stealthy deliberation, with minutes between steps, coming slowly nearer an unimpeded shot. Anticipation, and hopes finally realized, began to shake my heart, fear growing steadily within. I wondered now that the thunderous cacophony of my heart and breath would reveal my position, alert my prey, and destroy my hope for meat. He, however, was quite content to graze upon mountain grass along the southern rim, overlooking the vale, and was for now, oblivious to my stalk. With unsteady hands I fit shaft to string, slowly and silently, bending bow in deadly aim. At the right moment, I would surely pierce his flank and feast well upon his carcass; for now, all to do was wait!

A Single Tomorrow in a Land of Yesterdays

The Beast lifted his head, crowned in majestic fashion. Upon it he bore a most splendid, heavy rack of horns, worthy to grace any haughty hall of any haughty king. With insatiable greed, I strode forth in search of a more opportune shot. And as oft occurs in a moment of greed, caution and stealth were lost; unwarily I tread upon, and broke with loud report, a small branch. My moment had come! The Beast reacted, turning his flank toward me, providing me a shot of ease, and remained perfectly still—exceptionally calm!

For many days thereafter I puzzled at the events that followed. This beast—the prize I sought—had full and unhindered view of me as I rushed into a clearing, seizing my chance, and he yet remained motionless! It became suddenly—overwhelmingly—apparent that this was no chance meeting.

The Beast gazed with deep, penetrating eyes, and I wondered that this was sorcerer's work, for the enchantment I endured. I, the Hunter, seized, poised to deliver this beast's death, was held at peace by the eye of my Prey. The Hunted, seized, ready to bolt, held in check by sight of the Hunter. I did, discern, or maybe dream: the Beast did form a smile as my enchantment lingered. I do now deem that he not only knew what would befall, but that he wished it so. My heart raced with ambivalent confusion. What to do? I no longer wished him any harm, but that he would run free, that I could follow! Was it meant to be? My hands' strength was spent from holding bent bow for so long; the string sang as the shaft sprang free, sinking deep into his beautiful, sinuously rich, golden flank! My heart despaired; his blood flowed. And a single tear fell from his eye, splashing upon the cold, muddy ground below.

That tear was the Beast's only sign of pain. I fully expected him to drop immediately, for the arrow had surely struck a mortal wound. He, however, did naught but stand deathly still, returning my gaze, as the turf beneath him turned a crimson mire! I would have thought him dead, were it not for the mist his vaporous breath had formed.

"Now the deed is done. I must approach this animal king, repent and mend." This thought became a stirring within my soul. I attempted to undo the injury, striding forward slowly—penitently. This mysterious meeting of Hunter and Hunted became vastly more perplexing. For the Beast, pierced deeply in its vitals, bolted along the precipice edge, bearing west by the only path above the valley.

A great twilight settled heavily upon my soul; I knew not what perils lie ahead, and hunger grew giant-sized behind. With unnamed fear rising within, I gave chase at the best pace I could in that terrain. As I peered to my right into the valley, the rumors of its enchantment gave shadows root within my mind. With a deep drop into the vale a few feet to my right and a looming precipice (the feet of the mountains) within grasp of my left hand, I followed the trail of blood deep into the dark of night.

I debated myself aloud with these rumors: "O, to believe these foolish child's tales. Did I not outgrow that ages ago? What, do stories meant to drive children away also exhaust the courage within me?"

"Ere I saw it for myself. How might a beast surely struck with death, bleeding out more than any ever had, continue with unrelenting pace?"

"I am a simple man; I understand simple things. A sorcerer's handiwork would surely inscribe fear, but I endure no such emotion from this animal I pursue. The vale, contrarily, fills me with despair and dread, though it is beautiful to look upon; all will go ill if I journey there. I believe he leads somewhere with intent, and I mean to pursue." I spoke no more.

The path I followed was the only one that could be tread by man or beast, and darkness gave the blood its own light! To my astonishment, as the night grew dark, I could still perceive the splotches of blood many yards ahead. And when the moon shone upon it, it appeared as torchlight through a heavy mist for nearly a mile ahead. Sometime after midnight, I grew weary with travel and hunger, and sought some shelter for rest. The night grew cold, as I lay down just within an opening in the bluff to my left. The path had become very narrow indeed, and I slept uneasily within five feet of the descent into the vale. I awoke, hope renewed, at a nearby sound!

Had it been a footfall on the path, it would have scared me little; it came from within the cave. Rising to face it, my plan turned into an unforeseen mistake. There it was again—a high, shrill squeal of an animal sort. I grabbed my pack lying next to me, attempting to rise. At that moment, my mistake became suddenly clear; I saw I

A Single Tomorrow in a Land of Yesterdays

was no longer in the cave, but on the very verge of the valley wall! Again the squeal came—a vicious cackling—as I felt the crushing blow of the valley floor on my back!

There, lying upon my back, and the wreckage of my body, I saw the valley wall rise, sharply undercut; emotionless stone stared blankly back as my new captor. I was surprised by the depth of my fall (nearly twenty feet), and wondered that I still took breath, painful though it was. It seemed the floor itself had saved me—an exceedingly springy soft turf. My head swam, and I nearly swooned, as I rolled to survey the land.

I was in one of many glades of the vale, surrounded on three sides by very dense trees—trees whose tops had appeared blazed with the many autumn colors, and whose undersides were gloomy and gray. The towering stone face formed the fourth side of the glade. And above that wall rose a cheerful, glorious, and indescribably warm-looking mountain, Mount Veritheo. A heavy shadow, like a death-blanket, pervaded all the land I could see between the trees, except for the green, grassy glade in which I now buried my head. In fact, there existed such grayness in this land that time could hardly be discerned. Up on the wall it had been morning—the sun plainly visible above the eastern mountains—but here it seemed the twilight hour.

After a time, I had nearly forgotten my recent fright, and nearly passed into slumber when I heard many things! The first, gave me little bother; it was the sound of rustling leaves and branches. This would have been nothing at all, but for the plain truth that there was not even a slight breeze. Next, was something like a chattering of great numbers of animals. This, again, would have been nothing, but that, amongst the chattering, I heard rising and falling, the third easily distinguishable sound: the squeal I had heard atop the wall!

On my feet, I realized I had little defense to offer; my bow, unable to hurl any arrows, had broken in the fall. And my hunting knife was insufficient to slay the number of foes that waylaid me here. In the trees and on the ground, in every dark, impenetrable shadow a set of eyes shone back. I could but run, and that I did, as I had never done ere, or since. I stabbed, kicked, and ran over any eyes that dared come nigh, plodding north along the wall for a ways. I was a terror

A Single Tomorrow in a Land of Yesterdays

to my enemies, or I so thought, though they seemed contented to simply drive me in torturous fear, to and fro. My path, chosen by my foes amassing to one side, pushing me opposite, led northeast toward the center of the vale, near the bank of Canyon River.

Near that same bank, hope rekindled. I was now nearly spent by all recent activities, and strove ahead at a much slower pace; the eyes—eyes I had yet to discern the source of, out of the gray—grew in number, and came ever nearer. I was nearly overtaken, when I saw ahead on a rise of land, a defensible walled town, and with a burst of new strength I surged ahead into the town, turned, closed and barred the gate, and sank suddenly spent, back against the gate!

"Foes outside! Ready the defenses!" I cried in vain, seeing no one, "foes, foes are coming! Prepare the defenses. Defend the southern wall, foes have come." With woeful repetition I cried out, until hope had, at last, faded from recollection.

"Foes?" Came a reply, from a wizened, old man approaching from the town's center. He proceeded, talking as he drew slowly near, by help of a tall, dark staff. "Foes? We've not heard such foolishness here for an age. Nay, you are no fool, only a stranger, or lost traveler. What is this you rant about? Speak, I wish to know your story." Now, standing directly above me, I could see his dark eyes, his antique gray raiment, his enormous, sincere smile, his long, dark, flowing beard and hair, and his enormous staff. I could not discern if it was a weapon, or walking stick, or as it suddenly struck me: a sorcerer's staff. As he spoke again, my fear ebbed, and a great forgetfulness came upon me, "Tell me, child, for I wish to hear your story. From whence did you journey, and why? Speak. You are safe. This wall cannot be breached."

"S-s-sire, are-are-are y-you the s-ss-sorcerer?" I stammered on, "The old wizard who rules this vale? Many tales have I heard of y-you!"

Leaning down face-to-face, he smiled an extraordinary smile of simple pleasure, as the wrinkled lines of ancient ages—ages long forgotten—vanished from his visage. With a contagious laugh, he knocked my head playfully with his staff. In that moment, I was again beleaguered by an immense wave of forgetfulness. All recent fears, distresses, and memories faded to nothingness; I nearly lost all sense of self as he explained the situation.

"Sorcerer," he mocked, "nay, I am no sorcerer. You may call me —," here he paused, looking for the right word. He became obviously pleased with himself and continued, "Governor. Yes, Governor of this vale; I manage the people, resources, and the land. And you have yet to meet my pets. You shall love them."

At this, he gently set me on my feet and flung wide the gate. This dismayed me, though I was confounded as to why; and only now do I recall, for my eyes have been opened again—the spell broken! In rushed a thousand pair of shining eyes, each belonging to an apparition, or creature, somewhat like a monkey, or cat, or a mixture of the two! All shapes and sizes there were. Most were dark—gray to black—except for one little silvery fellow. It seemed that size with these creatures was proportioned to ugliness, so that the bigger they were the more ghastly they became—large shadowy devils!

The Governor instructed me to choose one for a companion, and sudden feelings of anxiety rushed over me. "Is this right?" I asked myself. "Why does this choice terrify me so?"

It was unavoidable; at this time a great gathering appeared out of many stone houses of the town, urging me to choose! Each person of this multitude was gaunt and upon every man, woman, and child these 'spectral monkeys' draped comfortably around the shoulders. I stood aghast. The mob becoming impatient, began chillingly chanting various phrases like: "Choose, choose now. We welcome you to our community. They are tame: they are safe. Choose, choose now."

It was then I chose this haunting specter, the one I deemed most harmless and most lovely. I chose the silvery creature with shining blue eyes. The little thing was well pleased, and was I, then.

The entire town began a celebration; there were many, many celebrations in those days. I inquired of all that were there and formed many lasting friends early in my stay. There were: James, Charlotte, Anthony, Timothy, Charles, Ardrew, and many more. Many tales could be told of these celebrations, or revelries, though I will tell only what I must. The Governor only appeared on the darkest of nights and to welcome any new stranger among us. The revelries included all kinds of pleasurable things: feasting, dances,

A Single Tomorrow in a Land of Yesterdays

ale consumption, debaucheries, and many more unmentionable deeds. These were ongoing most days and nights. Despite the constant consumption of food and drink, all feasters rapidly lost fat upon their bellies, and, in fact, the only things that grew were the 'spectral monkeys' perched upon our shoulders. It was during one such feast that we first perceived the Warrior.

He was a gallant man, heavily clad in shining armor—a fair, yet perilous man to behold. He walked where he pleased, though he never stayed—never reveled with us—and would speak earnestly to those with courage enough to endure his perilous sight. It was his third appearance that I would venture discourse with him, and I convinced Ardrew, James, and Charlotte to grudgingly accompany me. Oddly our spectral friends would not go near, chattering madly as we approached.

"Hail, friends," he removed his helm, "I bring gifts to you, and a summons, from Mount Veritheo. We are well met. I am Theonis."

I spoke first of my dear friends, "Theonis, well met, indeed. These are Charlotte, James, and Ardrew. We would ask: what purpose have you here?"

"To free all of this prison and to lead all to the Golden Stair, at the edge of Canyon River, to the very top of Mount Veritheo, to the Master Himself." At this Theonis bowed, pointing west to the Great Mount.

Ardrew dared to speak next, "You call this a prison. What know you of prisons? We are free to do as we wish, when we wish."

"What you wish, when you wish? And what would you venture to accomplish, without a heavy bulk upon your shoulders? You wither to nothingness while these beasts grow fat. And why? Look at what you've become, here in this glass!" He then handed each of us, in turn, a mirror. All but James, seeing our reflections, wept uncontrollably. "If you search for escape, seek out the glade at the northeast foot of Mount Veritheo, nigh the river bank. Fare thee well!" With that, he strode through the ever-barred North Gate of the town, toward the Governor's island.

"Rubbish." barked James, smashing the mirror while heading back to the revelry.

A Single Tomorrow in a Land of Yesterdays

The others looked much as I felt; we whispered back and forth as our companions perched heavily, once more, upon our thinning shoulders. I was surprised at the weight of mine, that his color now black, his eyes red, and his form ghastly! We conspired to find that Savior Glade that night during the height of revelry!

"I fear James will be lost forever," sobbed Charlotte, "he is dear to me, and I wish to bring him along."

"As do I!" Andrew and I chimed together.

"I will do all I can," I said compassionately, for I loved James, perhaps, dearest of all. "He will join us."

That night went as well as it could, for as short a time as it could. We meant to sneak out together; we did not. We wished to not be seen; we were. We wished for James to come willingly; he did not. We wished to leave our burdensome loads, our specters behind; we could not. The little success was that James accompanied me, we all made off in the right direction, and we were not yet followed. What transpired next, has embittered me with excessive anguish, beyond rays of hope.

James and I never reached the glade; we were waylaid in route. James bore the brunt of the attack, smitten to the ground by many ferocious specters—the largest and most treacherous of them all. They beat him and smashed him with rocks and clubs. Others bore me to the ground, content to restrain my rescue of James, and I watched as they destroyed him there. His blood ran and he was no more! Tears, thank the merciful heavens, blurred my eyes to the next horrific scene: many people I had known (from the town) began to tear and claw pieces of his body and devour it! Blood was everywhere. It ran from their mouths, down their hands, and all over their raiment. What is worse, they seemed to enjoy it as much as the revelries—venomous greed—fighting over him! I could say nothing, nor do anything; I was void!

Cast by my own choice—the beast upon my back—into the very fray, I fought and pleaded, to no avail! My hands were dipped in the great pool of blood, and forced toward my mouth! How could they do this? How could I do this? I fought and cried with the loudest voice, "No!" The blood had just touched my lips when my rescue arrived; I spat and fought with all strength. Five warriors, akin to

A Single Tomorrow in a Land of Yesterdays

Theonis, slew all the beasts, save my own. I slung him their way, and he also was struck down! My freedom came at a horrible price! Now I come to where I began this tale, with blood upon my hands—though it is not the end!

With my friend's blood on my hands, and repentance in my heart, the warriors and I raced to the glade. There Ardrew, Charlotte, and I were equipped just as they: in light, strong armor, an indestructible shield, helm, and a terrible swift and mighty sword. We were prepared for battle; my heart and hands cleansed.

With swift feet we raced to town, gathered all who would come freely, and set out for the River. Through the North Gate we sped, over the bridge, and onto the Governor's island. Here a battle of battles was fought; many fell deeds were done in single moments, upon the great horde of specters at the Governor's side. We fought with gallantry and unbelievable courage; Charlotte, Ardrew, and I slew countless beasts, heaping great injury upon the Governor himself. That great man was a foe with limitless strength and ability, but he now retreated to his dark and loathsome hold beneath the earth. And his vile blood was cleaned from all our swords! Victory was ours!

"To the Golden Stair!" We found ourselves bellowing in unison.

And to the Golden Stair we journeyed, upon the swift back of Canyon River. There, upon the Stair, the greatest mystery of all was revealed: I found the very thing I sought at the outset of my hunt! I now found the hart I had pierced and tracked, until I was cast into the Valley of the Shadow, knelt before us, bleeding heavily upon a great stair.

"Feast on me, my hungry children. Gain access to the Gate on Mount Veritheo. I die that you might live. Eat and be merry, for all is well. Be not afraid; lay aside all guilt!" This King of Beasts said this last, peering deep within me, and breathed his last!

We ate well and were satisfied, and my deep sorrow was inexplicably washed away. Awaking after a most restful sleep we found our vesture had changed to blazing white, and our armor, cleaned, shining like the sun.

"I wish to see that great Beast again," mourned Charlotte, as we approached the Gate atop Mount Veritheo.

"I believe we shall," I said, merrily. "I know we shall!"

Printed in the United States
62449LVS00002B/161